Gospel-Centered Youth Ministry

"Few of us take a trip without some kind of GPS device at our side. We need help navigating the route, the traffic, and the current road conditions, all in an effort to reach our final destination. In humble, authentic and truth-tested ways, *Gospel-Centered Youth Ministry* provides that level of clarity to those who are passionate about engaging, connecting, and discipling young people within the reach of their calling. With advice anchored in the timeless truth of God's Word, *Gospel-Centered Youth Ministry* delivers light to the unlit roads of working with young people. It underscores the priority of this mission, while amplifying the impact that an effective student ministry can have within a church community. Filled with wisdom, light, hope, and guidance, the contributors point to a clear objective—making lifelong followers of Jesus the Christ."

Dan Wolgemuth, President/CEO, Youth for Christ

"This book is both theologically insightful and practical . . . and a book about youth ministry must be both. This is a commendable resource for youth pastors, volunteers, students in training, and search teams looking for a youth pastor."

Jay S. Thomas, Lead Pastor, Chapel Hill Bible Church, Chapel Hill, North Carolina

"We see the lamentable statistics about younger people walking away from the church, despite every attempt over the last couple of generations either to turn up the cool factor or to fight the culture wars—or both. The contributors point to a better way. They have tested his gospel-centered approach and honed and refined it along the way. This book is not only a wake-up call, it is a practical guide for ministry to our younger brothers and sisters. I'll be recommending this book far and wide."

Michael Horton, J. Gresham Machen Professor of Systematic Theology and Apologetics, Westminster Seminary California; author, *Calvin on the Christian Life*

"You are holding a very helpful, straight-to-the-point examination of the fundamental how-to's in youth ministry. Covered here are the key areas of successful Christian youth leadership. Broad in scope but sharp in focus, this book will clearly help anyone who strives to have a ministry built on gold rather than straw."

Ken Moser, Assistant Professor of Youth Ministry, Briercrest College and Seminary; author, *Changing the World through Effective Youth Ministry*

"The contributors to this volume have reflected deeply on the nature and power of the gospel. Drawing from their years of experience, they have given us theologically rich and practical reflections on youth ministry that aim to exalt Christ, strengthen the whole church, and equip teenagers for ministry."

Mary Willson, Associate Director of Women's Initiatives, The Gospel Coalition

"Gospel-centered youth ministry is the need of the hour. It's rare to find a book that brings together expertise on everything from evangelism to small groups, from mission trips to social justice, but Cameron Cole and Jon Nielson have given us the perfect primer. I'm grateful for this book and look forward to putting it in front of my students!"

Alvin L. Reid, Professor of Evangelism and Student Ministry, Southeastern Baptist Theological Seminary; author, *As You Go: Creating a Missional Culture of Gospel-Centered Students*

"Here are 14 chapters written by 14 practitioners each with his or her own personality, writing style, and insight. Yet there is one focus—Jesus. For these writers, youth ministry is not only about teaching the teachings of Jesus, although that is important. Youth ministry is about making disciples—life-long learners personally following and growing in Jesus. These chapters are heart-felt and teen sensitive, with a profound respect for the gospel. That, plus a lot of practical insight make this a book worth having in your youth ministry library."

Terry Dittmer, National Director of Youth Ministry for the Lutheran Church Missouri Synod

"*Gospel-Centered Youth Ministry* is a substantial step in the right direction toward faithful discipleship of students. Not only should anyone in full time, part-time, or volunteer youth ministry purchase this book, but pastors and parents need to pick up a copy as well. Your church will be blessed by it."

John Perritt, Youth Director, Pear Orchard Presbyterian Church, Ridgeland, Mississippi

"Cameron Cole and Jon Nielson provide a clear vision of holistic ministry, encouraging and challenging readers to integrate the gospel as the center of their ministry with youth."

Brian H. Cosby, Pastor, Wayside Presbyterian Church, Chattanooga, Tennessee; author, *Giving Up Gimmicks: Reclaiming Youth Ministry from an Entertainment Culture*

Gospel-Centered Youth Ministry

A Practical Guide

Cameron Cole and
Jon Nielson, editors

FOREWORD BY COLLIN HANSEN

CROSSWAY®

WHEATON, ILLINOIS

Gospel-Centered Youth Ministry

Copyright © 2016 by Cameron Cole and Jon Nielson

Published by Crossway
  1300 Crescent Street
  Wheaton, Illinois 60187

All rights reserved. No part of this publication may be reproduced, stored in a retrieval system, or transmitted in any form by any means, electronic, mechanical, photocopy, recording, or otherwise, without the prior permission of the publisher, except as provided for by USA copyright law. Crossway® is a registered trademark in the United States of America.

Cover design: Tim Green, Faceout Studio

Shutterstock image #51178144

First printing 2016

Printed in the United States of America

Scripture quotations are from the ESV® Bible (The Holy Bible, English Standard Version®), copyright © 2001 by Crossway, a publishing ministry of Good News Publishers. Used by permission. All rights reserved.

All emphases in Scripture quotations have been added by the authors.

Trade paperback ISBN: 978-1-4335-4695-2
ePub ISBN: 978-1-4335-4698-3
PDF ISBN: 978-1-4335-4696-9
Mobipocket ISBN: 978-1-4335-4697-6

Library of Congress Cataloging-in-Publication Data
Gospel-centered youth ministry : a practical guide / Cameron Cole and Jon
  Nielson, editors ; foreword by Collin Hansen.
    pages cm
  Includes bibliographical references and index.
  ISBN 978-1-4335-4695-2 (tp)
    1. Church work with youth. I. Cole, Cameron, 1979– editor.
  BV4447 .G65   2016
  259'.23—dc23   2015016170

Crossway is a publishing ministry of Good News Publishers.

VP   26   25   24   23   22   21   20   19
14   13   12   11   10   9   8   7   6   5   4

Jon Nielson:
For my daughter Emilie.
May you know the riches of the glorious
gospel of our Lord Jesus Christ!

Cameron Cole:
To my gospel heroes,
Frank Limehouse
John Harper
Mark Upton
Gil Kracke
Thank you for leading me to the true gospel of grace.

Contents

Part 1

FOUNDATIONS FOR A GOSPEL-CENTERED YOUTH MINISTRY

Cameron Cole

This opening chapter articulates the heart behind this book: the conviction that the gospel of Jesus Christ must be at the center of all we do in ministry to youth.

Darren DePaul

This chapter argues for the centrality of intentional discipleship in youth ministry, and looks to Jesus Christ as the ultimate model for disciple makers.

Eric McKiddie

The method of teaching that will make the biggest long-term impact on students is expositional preaching that applies the gospel to everyday life.

Part 2

PRACTICAL APPLICATIONS FOR A
GOSPEL-CENTERED YOUTH MINISTRY

with the gospel of Jesus Christ, encouraged in faith, and challenged to serve and obey God with more worship and devotion.

Part 3

THE FRUIT OF A GOSPEL-CENTERED YOUTH MINISTRY

    Evangelism in the context of youth ministry is essential. Sadly, many youth ministers are failing to engage winsomely, lovingly, and truthfully with the youth culture as they share the life-giving message of the gospel of Jesus Christ. This chapter will give clear ideas and instructions for vibrantly engaging students and meeting them, where they are, with the good news of God's grace in Jesus Christ.

    Service to the poor, in the context of youth ministry, can be a confusing topic—and one that sends many youth ministers to extreme positions. There is, however, a gospel-centered way forward for thoughtful and real help for the poor in the name of Jesus Christ that will build, challenge, and grow our students as loving and generous followers of their Savior in this world.

    While short-term mission trips have gotten a bad rap in some Christian circles (often deservedly so), there is a way to engage in such trips for the glory of Jesus Christ, the advancement of his gospel, the discipleship of our students, and the genuine encouragement of believers in other parts of the world. This chapter gives us a way forward in carefully putting short-term trips to work in our ministries.

Foreword

Growing up, my family didn't make church a high priority. But I still took two years of confirmation classes and joined the youth group as a freshman in high school. I don't remember a lot of what was taught, and if I did, I'd probably disagree with much of it now. I know in one meeting we watched *The Seventh Sign*, starring Demi Moore, and I'm still confused as to how that movie was supposed to foster spiritual growth.

But one thing I saw in youth group began to change my life forever. For the first time I began to see peers who loved Jesus. I didn't know that was possible, because until then I only knew religion as an empty ritual. These peers introduced me to the crucified and risen Jesus. And I trusted him to forgive my sins and make a way to eternal life by the power of the Holy Spirit in the presence of my heavenly Father.

This experience has made me simultaneously thankful for youth groups and also concerned that they not lose their way. When we're so concerned with keeping the youth entertained or promoting a moral lifestyle, we can easily forget the message of first importance. The apostle Paul explains, "For by grace you have been saved through faith. And this is not your own doing; it is the gift of God, not a result of works, so that no one may boast" (Eph. 2:8–9).

In our work at The Gospel Coalition, "We have committed ourselves to invigorating churches with new hope and compelling joy based on the promises received by grace alone through faith alone in Christ alone." That's why I so eagerly commend *Gospel-*

Centered Youth Ministry: A Practical Guide. Over years of publishing these writers' works and watching their local church ministries, I have seen the hope and joy in their students as they receive grace through faith in Christ. What an eternal difference it would make if churches and youth groups around the world caught this vision to put the gospel at the center of their teachings, Bible studies, retreats, small groups, mission trips, and service projects.

Following this vision is simple, but it's not easy. There are many temptations and distractions. Youth workers, often young themselves and lacking ministry experience, get more feedback than counsel. This guide, then, offers an excellent start for any youth worker eager to make much of Jesus and to see students filled with everlasting hope and joy.

Collin Hansen
Editorial Director
The Gospel Coalition

Introduction

Many would say that youth ministry, a relatively young field, concluded its first generation near the turn of the twenty-first century. Experts invested much attention and energy in examining youth ministry's efficacy in forming young disciples with lasting faith. A disturbing dropout rate suggested that churches had failed miserably in their mission with young people.

The second wave of research assessed why the dropout rate among young people soared precipitously. Experts identified problems, including a lack of family involvement and the segregation of students from the multiple generations of the church. No factor appeared more influential, however, than the composite theology of youth ministry, which Christian Smith coined as *moralistic therapeutic deism.*

Smith defined moralist therapeutic deism in this way:

> Moralistic Therapeutic Deism is about inculcating a moralistic approach to life. It teaches that central to living a good and happy life is being a good moral person. That means being nice, kind, pleasant, respectful, responsible, at work on self-improvement, taking care of one's health, and doing one's best to be successful.[1]

One will be challenged to find a more direct antithesis and more powerful answer to this theological trend than the gospel of Jesus

---

[1] Christian Smith and Melinda Lundquist Denton, *Soul Searching: The Religious and Spiritual Lives of American Teenagers* (Oxford: Oxford University Press, 2009), 163.

Christ. The gospel proclaims what God has done *for* sinners above the moral performance *of* sinners. The gospel offers an inspiring call to live for God's kingdom, as opposed to living a shallow life focused on self-affirmation and self-centeredness. The gospel speaks of a God who is more than a fallback plan; he is a sovereign, living Lord actively involved with his people.

This book champions the gospel as the core of effective youth ministry. It argues that the message and reality of Christ's victory over sin and death should permeate every single facet of ministry to young people.

The theology sounds like a wonderful idea, but at the end of the day, kids will show up for Bible study and retreats, and we need to be prepared to practice the theology. The authors of this book believe that the gospel has practical implications for the way we conduct all areas of youth ministry.

This book lays out how the gospel relates to the major categories of youth ministry. The first section of each chapter provides philosophical and theological grounding for how the gospel informs a specific category of ministry. Then, each author explains how you can practically implement the gospel theology in that specific area of ministry in such a way that will help you both work out of the power of the cross and also explain to students the gospel purpose behind the activities.

We begin this book with what we consider to be the major foundations of effective youth ministry. These seven foundations include:

1. Gospel centrality
2. Discipleship
3. Expository teaching
4. Relationships
5. Community
6. Partnering with parents
7. Generational integration

Then we offer guidance on four practical elements of youth ministry, including:

1. Small-group Bible study
2. Volunteer training
3. Music
4. Retreats and events

Finally, while the first sections focus on our spiritual formation of students, the last chapters discuss the students' role in the redemptive mission of the church. We offer guidance on leading students in

1. Evangelism
2. Serving the poor
3. Short-term missions

Be encouraged: the work you are doing is important! God has placed you in a pivotal position in his church. We hope that these pages will aid you in leading a ministry that fosters lasting change in the lives of your students and brings light to this dark world.

Cameron Cole
May 2015

Part 1

FOUNDATIONS FOR A GOSPEL-CENTERED YOUTH MINISTRY

1

The Gospel at the
Heart of All Things

Youth Ministry Founded in the Gospel

Cameron Cole

What attracts people to ministry to youth? Why are they in this field? Is it the massive salaries? *Probably not.* Is it the promise of feeling impressive when they tell people at family gatherings or high school reunions about their career path? *Unlikely.* Is it easy hours and strict boundaries between work time and personal life? *Not a chance.*

Youth ministry can be a frustrating field of employment and a challenging volunteer calling. According to various studies, the normal tenure of a youth minister at a local church lasts approximately eighteen months.[1] Ministry to youth attracts a diverse collection of

---

[1] No comprehensive national survey exists but numerous regional or denominational studies consistently reveal an average tenure between 12–18 or 18–24 months.

people, in terms of personalities and backgrounds, but the motivation behind a person's entry into youth ministry is relatively universal. Certainly, it is not for the money, the status, or the ease. Youth ministers generally work countless hours for third-world pay while often being regarded as adult teenagers. They rarely sleep at night without at least one late-night text from a troubled or overly social teen. Then, after working to the brink of exhaustion much of the time, they field questions from parishioners like, "When you grow up, what do you think you want to do with your life?"

Given the lack of glory associated with ministry to youth and the personal emotional and physical cost of serving youth, a person who stays in the field—either as a volunteer or paid staff member—must see something extraordinarily precious that outweighs every difficulty. Two themes drive our mission and passion for ministry to youth:

> We long to see God heal, redeem, and free young people as they trust Jesus personally, and we long to see God birth something beautiful and redemptive in this broken world through their lives as they bear witness to their Savior.

Any person living in relationship with teenagers aches at the commonplace sufferings and intermittent traumas these young people endure. Witnessing the awkward, insecure, acne phases of middle school and the failed fashion experiments of high school makes me cringe. Seeing kids screaming for attention through provocative tweets and Facebook messages breaks my heart. Knowing the loneliness and alienation that comes in these years of self-doubt, religious questioning, and parental conflict causes me to lament. Yet these are the common experiences of almost every teen.

When I consider their exposure to divorce, pornography, drugs, alcohol, death, suicide, and violence, I long for the second coming of Jesus Christ. When I see the world in which these kids live, I begin to say to myself, *They're only children; this is just too much.* When I witness the suffering of teenagers, my passion for youth ministry explodes because I want their hearts healed. I want them to have hope. My commitment to youth ministry ignites because I know that news of what Jesus has done through his life, death, and resurrection contains the power to set them free. I know that God can bring them alive through faith in his Son.

Furthermore, when I see the world into which these children are headed, I long for redemption. I lament over the widespread addiction, broken sexuality, pervasive corruption, normalized self-absorption, flagrant injustice, unapologetic materialism, chronic depression, and utter despair. While the temptation arises to wallow in hopelessness and accept the status quo, I know that God intends to bring hope to those on earth through the activity of the Holy Spirit in the lives of his followers. The kids to whom I minister can be witnesses to God's redemption, sources of light, and agents of justice in a fallen, dark, desperate, crooked world. I want them to be people of the kingdom during their time in my ministry and every day after they leave the fold and enter the world. When I remember that, as a minister to youth, I am sitting in the most pivotal, influential position in the world to promote this global movement, I can be nothing but inspired. It's energizing to think of all God can do in the life of a person who lives for Christ and the kingdom from high school and on into college, marriage, family, and career.

I want this work of healing in young people's hearts and this passion for God's redemption in Christ to continue for the rest of their lives. I'm not looking for this to be the "Jesus phase" that they look back on as "cute" or "fun" when they enter their thirties. What a heartbreaking waste of time that would be! While I realize that not all the kids in my ministry will surrender their lives to Christ, I long for the currents of God's work in the kids to flow when they are eighteen, twenty-eight, and seventy-eight.

Given that youth ministry focuses on *lasting redemption*, what catalyzes transformation in the lives of teenagers? Is it close friendships, fun games, moral training, positive role models, community service, or uplifting music? Not really. *Perhaps the most important thing a person ministering to youth can possess is an accurate appraisal of the fundamental problem in both people and the world and a clear understanding of the way God can restore them both.*

The Problem and the Solution

My most influential mentor in my early years of serving in youth ministry impressed upon me an important maxim: "Theology drives methodology." This is a jargon-filled way of saying that what you do in ministry reflects what you believe.

Perhaps critics of youth ministry have used too much hyperbole and generalization in characterizing the practice of youth ministry. Stereotypically, the practice of youth ministry included entertaining events, lessons on moral behavior, an emphasis on good spiritual habits, and efforts to inspire students toward deeper commitments to God in the context of a group of friends. In playful terms, youth ministry is dodgeball, abstinence, and pep rallies with your buddies in the name of God. While this description is an exaggeration, some truth lies beneath the stereotype. (If you're starting to roll your eyes and say, "Not this again!" . . . stay with me. There is extremely good news coming.)

Traditionally, youth ministry methodology demonstrated a specific theology about kids' biggest problem. It suggested that kids lack both proper knowledge about moral Christian living and sufficient motivation to adhere to the standards. The kids would do right if they just knew how to obey God, and if they had consistent reinforcement to "be good Christians." Therefore, youth ministries functioned to educate students on Christian behavior and exhort kids to live for God. This belief may have manifested itself practically through frequent messages centered on behavior, worship designed to generate emotional responses, and exhortations for increased effort in the pursuit of moral Christian living.

Presently, I think youth ministries are moving away from these methods. Due to the volumes of research suggesting that the moralistic, emotional, entertaining approach to youth ministry has had little to no efficacy in creating lasting followers of Jesus, many youth pastors have put the dry ice machine in the church attic and toned down the underage drinking speeches. Still, I am not confident that youth ministry as a whole has identified the substance of what God uses to change lives.

The kids of today have the exact same problem as their great-great-great-great-great-grandparents, Adam and Eve. Humanity has not fundamentally changed since the days of the garden of Eden. Any person ministering to youth can understand the three fundamental issues underlying every teenager's problem with an investigation of Genesis 3. There we find the record of Adam and Eve eating from the tree of knowledge of good and evil, in disobedience to God's word. Let's think together about this account for a few moments.

Problem 1: Source of Truth

Teenagers lack an accurate understanding of the source of truth. The Serpent's initial act of deceit in Genesis 3:1 comes when he asks, "Did God *actually say*, 'You shall not eat of any tree in the garden'?" God had spoken clearly to Adam and Eve in Genesis 2:17, telling them that eating the fruit of the tree of the knowledge of good and evil will result in death. Eve even acknowledges this. Their downfall begins, however, with this statement in Genesis 3:6: "When the woman saw that the tree was good for food, and that it was a delight *to the eyes*." Eve shifts from operating under the authority of what God verbally had revealed to her and now uses her own senses and judgment for her view of morality, herself, and God.

Many times, teenagers express hesitation about God based on the suffering they see in the world. They frequently question his goodness based on disappointments they have experienced in their lives. They often open statements about moral convictions with "I think" and "I feel." Like every other human being, they naturally derive their views on truth through their own experiences and observations. Rarely would a person confidently consider God good and just if they based their views on their own experience, given the normal pains in life and evils in the world. Would any teenager abstain from sex until marriage if left to his or her own rationality?

The first part of the solution to this fundamental problem involves pointing students to the authoritative sources, Jesus and the Bible, which accurately represent God, man, and truth. Youth ministry hoping to make lasting change needs to constantly hold Jesus up "as the image of the invisible God" (Col. 1:15). Christ-centered ministry moves students toward embracing the goodness and holiness of God. Furthermore, effective ministry bases its lessons and teachings on Scripture. It moves students toward a worldview grounded in the truth God has revealed in the Bible.

Problem 2: View of Self

The second problem plaguing all teens is a false view of self. The Serpent sold Adam and Eve the lie that they could "be like God" (Gen. 3:5). After eating from the tree, the first couple demonstrated this distorted belief through their actions, which screamed independence. First, when they realize they have sinned and created damage, the wounded couple takes matters into their own hands by crafting leaves to cover their shame (Gen. 3:7). They did not believe that they needed God; they could handle this problem on their own. Then, when God confronted them about their misdeed, Adam and Eve both shifted blame. Adam says, "That woman made me do it," and Eve, "It's the serpent's fault" (see Gen. 3:11–13). They behaved as if they were above accountability and did not have to answer to God.

The view of the human condition depicted in Scripture is not a pretty picture. Jesus himself referred to his disciples—the cream of the Christian crop—as "evil" in Matthew 7:11. Christ told Nicodemus in John 3:19 that, "people loved the darkness rather than the light because their works were evil." In Romans, Paul said that all "have sinned and fall short of the glory of God" (Rom. 3:23). The prophet Jeremiah took it to another level, saying that "The heart is deceitful above all things, and desperately sick; who can understand it?" (Jer. 17:9). Wow! This is brutal news.

Before things become too depressing, we must remember that human depravity, although deep, has simple roots: humans think they can be God. Teenagers, like all people, naturally believe they can live their lives, independent of God and without his help. Effective youth ministry does not need to beat teenagers over the head about their "wickedness." It simply needs to inform and remind students that they are made to live in a dependent relationship with God, and that they naturally defy this need. It must help them understand that all of their sin originates from attempting to be the lord in their own lives, rather than allowing Jesus to be their King. But let's be frank: sugarcoating the reality of human sin is a major disservice to kids. It's like telling a person diagnosed with cancer that it is only a cold.

Problem 3: View of God

Finally, the third issue plaguing all teens is a false view of God. The Serpent created seeds of doubt in Adam and Eve when he told them that God was lying—they would not surely die by eating from the tree (Gen. 3:4). Then he led them to believe that God was holding out on them, because he knew that they would be "like God" if they ate the fruit (Gen. 3:5). The Serpent portrayed God as a liar who withholds goodness from his children. Adam and Eve took the bait and ate from the tree. After their fatal deed, they demonstrated their new theology in the way they reacted to God's entrance into the garden. What did they do? They ran and hid, and then they lied. Their behavior exhibited their belief that God was one who would not forgive and whom they could not trust. God was bad according to this new "theology."

Perhaps the most important element of effective youth ministry, then, is proclaiming the goodness and love of God. No teenager will entrust his or her life to a person they cannot trust. However, who can resist trusting and knowing the *true* God of the Bible? He is "slow to anger and . . . forgiving" (Num. 14:18). He "waits to be gracious . . . and therefore he exalts himself to show mercy" (Isa. 30:18). His works are perfect and he is without flaw (Deut. 32:4). God is the One who teenagers can cast their cares upon because he cares for each one of them (1 Pet. 5:7). Knowing the true character of God heals the teenage heart, as young people see his love poured out at the cross of Jesus.

The problem of every teenager runs incredibly deep. The false beliefs that underlie their sin and suffering are deeply ingrained in their hearts from birth. Thinking that morals and motivational speeches will fix this problem is like believing a Band-Aid will heal a broken leg or that aspirin will cure cancer. Teenagers need a total overhaul of their belief systems. Above all, teenagers, like every person, need God to rescue, revive, and re-create them, as they repent of sin and entrust their lives to Jesus as Savior and Lord.

The Change Agent

Youth ministry seeking lasting changes must flow out of the theology of the cross. The cross presents a picture of a just, loving, and revealed God. Jesus Christ, God in human flesh, bears the full punishment for the sins of God's people in their place, in order to bring salvation.

God does not remain hidden. He exposes himself fully in the crucified Christ, whom we learn of through his Word, the Bible. He reveals himself as one in love with his people in his incarnation and through the holy inspired Word.

The cross tells honestly the depth of man's problem with sin. Man's sin issue is so deep that God himself would have to leave heaven, endure torture on a cross, and experience eternal judgment to fix it. That's not a skinned-knee-level problem; that's an issue of epic proportions. It is a problem only fixed by the power of God, not by the best efforts of people.

Finally, the cross sings the song of the immeasurable love of

God. His love for man is so great and passionate that he, in fact, would leave paradise to endure such suffering for his beloved people. He would take on hell to rescue his people from it. The cross is the most passionate, determined love story of all time.

This theology of the cross captures what Christians refer to as the gospel. In Greek, *gospel* means "good news" and, in the original cultural context, often referred to a comforting announcement of victory in either battle or politics. While many people define the gospel in various ways, these definitions generally revolve around God's victory over sin and death in the life, death, and resurrection of Jesus. This victory not only redeems sinful people who put their faith in Jesus, but it also extends to God's broader work of restoring the fallen world through the Holy Spirit—a restoration that one day will be completed in God's creation of a new heaven and new earth.

The reason the authors of this book consider gospel centrality so critical to youth ministry is that it addresses the heart of students—their true problems and their greatest eternal potential. Rules, motivational speeches, fun, and friends have no power to heal hearts and revive lives like the good news of Christ's completed work. When we take ministry back to the gospel, we are connecting students with the power of Jesus's cross and resurrection. God can accomplish the purpose of ministry to youth (*lasting change*) through the gospel as they believe in Jesus and follow him forever.

Given that this book focuses on connecting all facets of youth ministry to the gospel, I want to conclude this chapter by sharing personal stories that shed light on the practical implications of the gospel and express some of the passion fueling these pages. Too often "gospel people" (myself included) use the term flippantly without describing its concrete applications in life and ministry. Furthermore, we fail to define what aspects of the gospel we are referring to when discussing it.

In these final three sections of the chapter, I describe three aspects related to the gospel: (1) the gospel and salvation, (2) the gospel and grace, and (3) the gospel and redemption. I have seen

God redeem, heal, free, inspire, and comfort me through the gospel. He has brought life and fruit to my ministry that I never thought possible. I hope these stories and explanations will encourage and awaken readers to the rich possibilities of what God can do through the gospel, in a way that will breed hope, faith, and worship to Jesus.

The Gospel and Salvation

While my passion for sharing the gospel began at a Disciple Now weekend at First Baptist Church of Birmingham in January 1993, it climaxed in a children's hospital resuscitation room on November 11, 2013. On that morning, my wife called me in utter panic to share the horror that our three-year-old son, Cam, had stopped breathing and had no pulse when she checked on him in his bed that morning. I raced from a youth campout to a children's hospital in time for the doctors to tell us they had exhausted all efforts: our baby boy was dead.

As we went to the resuscitation room to see our son for the last time, my wife, Lauren, and I recalled our conversation with Cam the previous afternoon. Cam told us that he wanted to go "visit" Jesus, and he suggested that we hop in the car. We explained to Cam that Jesus was with us now in the Holy Spirit and that we would see Jesus face-to-face when God called us to heaven. He, with a supernatural focus in his eyes, then asked, "Will I see Adam and Eve in heaven?" (Pretty impressive for a three-year-old.) Lauren and I discussed and told Cam that, indeed, God appeared to forgive Adam and Eve's sin in Genesis 3. Cam replied, "I'm not going to eat that apple. I not eat from that tree." I told Cam that everyone "eats from the tree" and disobeys God; that's why Jesus came. Cam ended this conversation by saying, "Jesus died on cross, Jesus died my sins." The next morning, Cam passed into God's kingdom.

While the pain of losing a child is inconceivable, what an incredible comfort my wife and I have in knowing that our son professed faith in Jesus and his work on the cross—the day before his death.

My wife and I can live with the certain hope of our reunion with Cam in heaven. While I have had a passion for proclamation of the gospel of salvation since the seventh grade, never has its beauty and power been so real or palpable as the day we said good-bye to Cam. In discussing the gospel of salvation, I refer to the message that God sent Jesus into the world to live perfectly and die on a cross for sinners, and rise again for their eternal life, in order that those who receive Christ by faith may live eternally in heaven with God. The gospel of salvation points to the historic, complete, atoning work of Jesus and the mandate to spread this word of good news.

The proclamation of the gospel of salvation constitutes one of the most pivotal functions of youth ministry. So often in youth ministry, we can become enchanted with good, but not ultimate, matters. Missional living, social justice, and Christian community all represent wonderful things that I desire students in my ministry to embrace. At the same time, we never should neglect the essential duty and blessed opportunity of making students aware of their need for salvation and offering Jesus as the certain comfort and solution to the only A-list problem life presents: What will happen to people when they die?

When we approach ministry to youth with this biblical clarity, the stakes are raised and our vocation takes on substantial meaning. Our work involves the eternal condition of the souls of the precious students whom God has shared with us. Regardless of the impression society may have of a youth minister, we know that we engage in serious business each day. We may visit amusement parks, play lots of Frisbee, and send thousands of texts per month, but do not be mistaken: when a youth worker or volunteer focuses on the gospel of salvation, his or her time addresses the single most critical matter in any person's life.

Ministry to youth with the gospel at the center means we frequently take the opportunity to proclaim the good news of salvation through Christ. We pray fervently that the Holy Spirit will work in the hearts of our students. We equip volunteer leaders and students to share the gospel in their world. We go out into the world—including our cities and foreign lands—and proclaim Christ by word and deed.

The Gospel and Grace

While I finished high school with a developed theology for the gospel of salvation, I had no concept of the gospel of grace. My general theology revolved around accepting Jesus for salvation, sharing Christ with others, and then trying really, really hard for God out of my own strength, using Jesus as my role model. In fact, even though I started following Jesus in the third grade, I had to look up the definition of "grace" in a dictionary, while writing a paper during my third year of college at Wake Forest.[2]

My personal theology translated into a life of performance—an exhausting treadmill. As a senior in high school, I took five AP classes, taught myself an additional AP course, attended eight swim practices per week, wrote for the newspaper staff, served on the state board of the Key Club, and held offices as vice president of the student body and vice president of the Honor Society. College was no different. I finished Wake Forest (often referred to as "Work Forest") as a double major in three years, while starting a de facto nonprofit. I completed a master's degree during my fourth year.

No one would be surprised to discover that this exhausting pace wreaked havoc on my mental health. While teaching in inner-city Charlotte during my first year out of graduate school, I started to have problems with short-term memory. I lost my keys daily and often forgot my train of thought midsentence. Then I experienced trouble sleeping. The problem escalated when a phobic dread of returning to the school would set in as soon as I left the campus each evening.

I scheduled a meeting with my pastor, Mark Upton, of Hope Community Church, to discuss my turmoil. Mark informed me

---

[2] I think I should note that my youth ministers talked about unconditional love a great deal; the words simply did not land in my heart until my early twenties.

that I had two major problems. First, he said that the catalogue of symptoms I described sounded like the precursors of a nervous breakdown. He said that I needed to consult a physician and seriously consider resigning from my job. The second issue, he said, was that I did not know the gospel of grace. He did not doubt my salvation or sincerity as a follower of Jesus. He told me these words that changed my life forever:

The gospel is rest. The gospel means Jesus carries the burden of your life. The gospel means you will never have to prove yourself again, because Jesus has proven you on the cross.

He explained that the same dynamic truth underlying my salvation—my need to rely on God for grace and God's amazing generosity—extended to all facets of my life. Growing in Christ meant growing in the understanding of my powerlessness as a sinner and increasing in the practice of seeking God's help for everything.

At the end of the meeting, we prayed about whether I should quit my job. Two days later I had a panic attack, which resulted in my inability to speak for four weeks or to read for eight weeks straight. Needless to say, I resigned. I spiraled into a deep depression for six months, but it was wonderful because I discovered freedom through the gospel like never before. God began to heal me through the message of his grace and love.

When we refer to the gospel of grace in this book, we refer to the good news that Jesus's death on the cross does not simply seal sinners for eternal life in heaven (although it certainly does do that for those who trust him as Savior and Lord and repent of sin), but also extends to all areas of a Christian's life. Consequently, sanctification involves a person becoming more like Christ—not only through daily repentance—but ultimately through the work of the Holy Spirit and through increased dependence on God's grace in every category of life.

Perhaps the greatest flaw in youth ministry is the historic absence of the gospel of grace. Ministry to youth ordinarily has preached salvation well. However, after students become believers, too often the dynamic shifts to one of moralism with the primary focus centering on sexual purity, underage drinking, and general "niceness." Too often I encounter burned out former church kids who walked away from years in youth ministry with an understanding of Christianity as simply another avenue by which one can try to be a good person. The burden of performance broke their backs and damaged their faith. What a tragedy!

Good secular organizations, like the Boy Scouts, sports teams, and public schools, encourage moral performance and character building. Christian youth workers need to understand that our unique asset in seeing lives changed is the gospel of grace. When teenagers grasp that God loves them perfectly and permanently in spite of their sins, there is great hope of transformation. When a kid adopts a gospel rhythm of life, whereby he or she sees the need for God and depends on his grace, God can bring immeasurable healing, freedom, and fruit. The gospel of grace must appear over and over again in our teaching and discipleship of young people.

The Gospel and Redemption

In 2006 I took a dozen students to New Orleans in the months following Hurricane Katrina. On the first evening, we drove into the Lower Ninth Ward, the area of most dire devastation from the epic storm. Silence and tears filled the van during the drive through the abandoned neighborhood. Neither the kids nor the adult leaders could fathom the destruction or the despair.

The next morning I attended the pastors' meeting, where over sixty leaders from around the country received marching orders and offered fervent prayers. Our group was working alongside over twelve hundred adults and teenagers who had descended on the city for the sake of seeing New Orleans revived after the hurricane. As we drove to our work site, where we would be demolishing the moldy interior of a widow's home, we called the homeowner. She had been relocated to a government nursing home in Oklahoma after the storm and awaited volunteers to clear the moldy contents of her home, which had sat under seven feet of water during the storm. Her glee in hearing that help had arrived inspired our students.

As I entered the house that first morning, several students and I immediately vomited because of the appalling smell in the home, which had sat closed up for months with festering mold. The ministry called us to remove everything within the home until nothing remained but the concrete slab, the roof, and the studs. All furniture, carpet, Sheetrock, and insulation had to go, so that new construction could begin. The kids put on their masks and goggles and worked tirelessly in the oppressive summer heat for three days. Each morning and evening the kids would call the sweet widow to let her know of the progress. With each hour of work, the waste was removed and the offensive smell reduced until the final day when the odor had been eradicated.

The inspiring project broadened my understanding of the gospel. In response to their appreciation for Jesus, our students loved this elderly woman whom they talked to on the phone each day. Along with dozens of other groups in the neighborhood, our kids dove into the darkness and decay and brought light and life. They were witnessing God redeem this home, this woman's life, and this city.

The smell told the whole story. When we arrived, there was a smell of death and decay. Through this mission God made the home clean again. It was a tangible portrait of transformational work God does, not only in the hearts of his people, but also in the world. This service itself is not the gospel per se, but it reflected the broader redemption God is doing in the world through Christ. The students' response to the gospel, in serving this woman, bore witness to the eternal redemption that their Savior brings to lost and broken lives.

Scripture speaks of a total, cosmic work that flows out of the cross. In Ephesians 1, Paul tells of the will and purpose of God "to unite all things in him, things in heaven and things on earth" (Eph. 1:10). Paul writes again in Colossians 1 that God purposed through Christ "to reconcile to himself all things, whether on earth or in heaven, making peace by the blood of his cross" (Col. 1:20). To reduce the gospel only to the salvation of souls shortchanges the magnitude and breadth of the work of Jesus. God's vision for salvation and redemption encompasses both the souls of people and everything in the universe. One day, God will make all things new—glorified people, as well as a new heavens and new earth.

Youth ministry with a complete view of the gospel places the cross at the foundation of its missional endeavors. Students do not simply do mission trips and service to the poor because they represent good deeds to which Scripture calls us. A response to the gospel drives them. Youth workers constantly should remind kids that their lives and service are a part of God's total work to redeem fully the whole world for the sake of Christ.

Moving Forward

This chapter captures the heart behind this book. It argues that the gospel serves as the catalyst for fostering lasting change in the lives of teenagers and in the redemption of the world. It encourages youth workers and volunteers to place the gospel at the center of their ministries. But what does that mean? How does that practically occur in a ministry? The rest of this book points the way to solving these questions for your particular ministry.

More on . . . the Gospel

D. A. Carson and Timothy Keller, *The Gospel as Center* (Crossway, 2012).

Greg Gilbert, *What Is the Gospel?* (Crossway, 2010).

John Piper, *God Is the Gospel* (Crossway, 2005).

2

Making Disciples Who Make Disciples

Discipleship in Youth Ministry

Darren DePaul

The focus of this chapter is discipleship in the context of youth ministry. The content of this chapter is by no means exhaustive, but it will hopefully serve as a guide for you, as a leader in the church, to relationally and effectively disciple young people. Here is my basic, biblical assumption: *the primary role of the youth pastor and the student ministry in the local church is to make disciples of Jesus Christ.*

I must be clear from the outset that I do not believe in one particular model of discipleship, other than the one we find demonstrated in the person and work of Jesus Christ. The programs that we enable, along with how we relate to different students, will adapt and change, but Jesus Christ and his call to make disciples will not. Jesus is our model, not merely as a guide but as the personification of discipleship. He not only called and led the disciples and others to himself, but loved them, taught them, trained them, equipped them, and sent them out to do as he had done . . . make disciples (Matt. 28:19; Mark 11:17; 16:15–16).

Before we move into the main content of the chapter, we must first provide a simple definition of a disciple. A disciple is a lifelong learner who is following and growing in relationship with Jesus Christ. This consistent following and growing in Christ is essential because it means that the disciple is personally experiencing the love and grace of Jesus and then, just as Jesus did, giving that love and grace to others in word and deed. Unfortunately, as has been outlined in many books over the last several years, many churches have failed at "making" disciples because the central focus has been only on the teachings of Jesus rather than on the importance of personally following and growing in Jesus. As Jonathan Dodson noted, "Gospel-centered discipleship is not about how we perform but who we are—imperfect people, clinging to a perfect Christ, being perfected by the Spirit."[1] The focus then is not only on knowing about Jesus, but on "clinging" to him and "being" with him. Jesus modeled this (John 10), the disciples did this, and we are called to the same as we minister to young people.

Our youth ministries should be focused on making disciples who will in turn make disciples. Here is where we must be honest with ourselves as people who lead young people. We must ask: Is the point of our youth ministry the program or the people? Is it about growing followers of Jesus or about the great American youth ministry dream of big programs and personal accolades?[2] For the Pharisees, their mission focused on programs, the outward appearance, and a legalistic religion that brought death instead of life. Jesus, on the other hand, was relational. He focused on the heart of the indi-

---

[1] Jonathan Dodson, *Gospel-Centered Discipleship* (Wheaton, IL: Crossway, 2012), 18.
[2] Please see an article I wrote for Rooted Ministry: Darren DePaul, "Letting Go of the American Youth Ministry Dream," Rooted Ministry (blog), April 29, 2013, http://rootedministry.com/articles/letting-go-american-youth-ministry-dream.

vidual person and, in the midst of relationship, challenged him or her to abandon idols for the sake of an abundant life through faith in him. And Jesus said to all, "If anyone would come after me, let him deny himself and take up his cross daily and follow me" (Luke 9:23). Those words are just as challenging now as they were two thousand years ago when Jesus first delivered them, and in no way have they lost their value or relevance.

As you think about your own growth as a disciple and how you're leading the young people in your ministry, think about these words from Tom Sine, "Jesus expects those who follow Him to be as extreme as His first followers were in putting aside every lesser thing and making this business of being a disciple a whole-life proposition."[3] This is, in other words, a call to believe Jesus and also to *embrace* him personally as Savior and Lord. Discipleship involves knowing about Jesus . . . and also knowing Jesus.

We must remember as youth leaders that discipleship is a journey—a long journey. Large groups, small groups, one-on-one meetings, mission trips, and the like all play a part in that journey for our students, but the focal point must always be Jesus. We should be teaching, leading, showing, and modeling to our young people that being a disciple is not about a program or our personality, but rather about following Jesus in all of life. Francis Chan stated this well when he wrote, "Making disciples is far more than a program. It is the mission of our lives. It defines us. A disciple is a disciple maker."[4]

As we pour into the lives of our students we must also remember that discipleship is a purposeful process. Simply because a student "shows up" doesn't mean he or she is following Jesus, or even has a context to know what that means.[5] My hope in this short chapter is to address a few areas that will help us as we consider how to

---

[3] Tom Sine, *Taking Discipleship Seriously: A Radical Biblical Approach* (Valley Forge, PA: Judson, 1985), 8.

[4] Francis Chan, *Multiply: Disciples Making Disciples* (Colorado Springs: Cook, 2012), 31.

[5] For a helpful article on discipleship involving the church, see Godwin Sathianathan, "Grow a Disciple-Making Culture in Your Church," The Gospel Coalition (blog), February 26, 2013, http://thegospelcoalition.org/blogs/tgc/2013/02/26/how-to-grow-a-disciple-making-culture-in-your-church/.

purposefully disciple the students whom the Lord has placed in our lives, for the glory of our Lord and Savior.

The Purpose of Discipleship

Discipleship in the context of youth ministry is leading, teaching, and modeling to our students what it means to be a lifelong learner who is following and growing in Jesus Christ. While discipling, we must remember that right information and teaching is not an adequate strategy to make disciples.[6] We must indeed teach the Bible, theology, and doctrine clearly and effectively, but we cannot lose sight of the intensely relational aspect to discipleship. While our programs are of some value, we should view them not as the end but as the means to connect with students relationally, pushing them to know and grow in relationship with Jesus Christ. Several years ago, I read Steve Shadrach's book *The Fuel and the Flame*. He wrote something that changed the way I thought about discipleship: "If you want to see your campus ablaze for Christ, purpose-driven, love-filled relationships will have to permeate your life and ministry. Why? Because discipleship is a combination of direction and affection."[7] For so long, I focused on direction in discipleship but neglected the affection. We can't simply say we're about relational ministry; we actually have to *be* about those relationships.

We must constantly examine our hearts and our ministries and ask the hard question: Are we making disciples? That is the command that Jesus has put before us. He made disciples and commands us to follow his lead and "make disciples" (Matt. 28:19). Jesus "made" a handful of disciples and then they went and made disciples. Jesus calls us to do the same today, and if our ministries do not have disciple making as their goal, we may find that we are dangerously out of step with Jesus himself!

The underlying purpose of relational youth ministry is to connect young people to Jesus—making disciples who will make dis-

---

[6] Mike Breen, *Building a Discipling Culture* (Pawleys Island, SC: 3DM, 2011), 26.
[7] Steve Shadrach, *The Fuel and the Flame: 10 Keys to Ignite Your College Campus for Jesus Christ* (Waynesboro, GA: Authentic Lifestyle, 2003), 101.

ciples. Yet, with so many demands on us through programming, staff meetings, and other responsibilities, our relationships with students can suffer. Relationships mattered to Jesus and they should matter to us and to our ministries.

PRACTICAL CONSIDERATIONS FOR DISCIPLESHIP IN YOUTH MINISTRY

A Pattern for Discipleship

Through his life and ministry, Jesus provided a pattern for us to emulate as we engage in relational ministry. He showed us how to effectively disciple others by initiating, identifying, and invading the lives of those that the Father put before him.[8] We see this in the beginning of his ministry in the calling of the first disciples (Matt. 4:18–22; Mark 1:16–34; Luke 5:1–11), to the end of his life and ministry as he hung on the cross and ministered to the repentant criminal (Luke 23:41–43). While there are countless accounts in the life and ministry of Jesus where we see him initiating, identifying, and invading the lives of people, for the sake of space we will focus on one transforming passage: John 4 and the account of the woman at the well.[9]

Initiate

In the beginning of the story in John 4, Jesus had been in Judea, and it was time for him to move on to Galilee. As Jesus began the journey to Galilee, John wrote that Jesus *"had to pass through Samaria"* (4:4). Now, Jesus didn't technically need to "pass through" Samaria, which was an area detested by the Jews; the need was

---

[8] I first learned of the language of initiate, identify, and invade from Pastor Andy Lewis, the lead pastor at Mitchell Road Presbyterian Church in Greenville, South Carolina, a church I served at as the director of youth and family ministry for nearly eight years.

[9] A portion of the "initiate, identify, and invade" section first appeared in an article I wrote for Rooted Ministry: Darren DePaul, "Jesus and That Kid: The Woman at the Well," Rooted Ministry (blog), August 12, 2013, http://rootedministry.com/articles/jesus-and-kid-woman-well.

based on God's divine purpose. As Rodney Whitacre noted, "There is no geographical necessity for going through Samaria. The necessity is due to God's plan. . . . The Father was sending Him there to look for those who would worship Him in spirit and truth (4:23)."[10]

Passing through our ministries each week are students the Lord is putting before us and calling us to engage. He continues to look for those *who would worship him in spirit and truth,* and our calling is to engage with those students relationally. Our disciple making begins with listening and being open, just as Jesus was, to those divine meetings that the Lord is putting in our lives.

Tired from his travels, Jesus stopped and sat at a well in Samaria. As Jesus was sitting there, a *woman from Samaria came to draw water* and he asked her for a drink. On the surface, her coming to the well does not seem that unusual to us, but context is key; the text says she was there at the sixth hour, which is noon. In that day, no woman would go out at noon to draw water for her family unless she was a social outcast (Gen. 24:11; 29:7).

The Samaritan woman went to the well when she knew she would be alone. Her life was messy and her reputation in the community was nothing less than scandalous. Jesus initiated a relationship with this woman, whom any self-respecting religious man would have avoided, and spoke truth into her life. Jesus patiently explained to her, despite her confusion and lack of understanding of his words, that there was a real, living water available to her—living water that provides eternal and everlasting fulfillment (John 4:13–15).

With Jesus as our model, we see that making disciples starts with initiation. Just as God's plan was for Jesus to initiate with the woman at the well, his plan for us is to initiate with the students in our ministries and the community. As you picture the faces of those in your youth ministry, or those with whom you have regular connections, ask yourself if you are initiating with them. Are you engaging them in intentional relational ministry? Discipleship

---

[10] Rodney A. Whitacre, *John*, IVP New Testament Commentary (Downers Grove, IL: IVP Academic, 2010), 101.

begins with engaging and connecting with the students who have been placed in your life and ministry . . . that's initiating, and that's following Jesus as our model. Even more, that's following him personally. Our calling as youth leaders is to initiate with students, to break down the walls of the culture and subcultures, and bring forth the gospel—the overwhelming, unchanging, and incomprehensible love and grace of Jesus Christ, which alone can bring salvation, change, and hope for students' lives.

Jesus initiated with the woman at the well, and though she was confused and lacked understanding of Jesus's words, she desired this living water. The woman said to Jesus, *"Sir, give me this water, so that I will not be thirsty or have to come here to draw water"* (John 4:15). Our efforts at making disciples who will make disciples must go beyond our Wednesday night games and our attractional approach to youth ministry. For some of us, this means that our focus must change "from putting on attractional events to creating attractional communities."[11] Like Jesus, we must be on mission to initiate; we must engage, and we must show and lead our students to the living water that can only be found in the Lord.

For some youth pastors and leaders, this will mean getting past personal reservations, insecurities, and feelings of awkwardness. We must remember that, ultimately, the ministry to which we are called is not about us! We must *initiate* relationships with students; their reception of the true gospel may depend on it!

Identify

While Jesus initiated with the woman at the well, he was not interested in a mere conversation about well water. Jesus had every intention of identifying her deepest need for the freedom and salvation that could only be found in him. To make the woman aware of her sin, Jesus spoke right to her heart: *"Go, call your husband, and come here"* (John 4:16). The woman attempted to

---

[11] Tim Chester and Steve Timmis, *Everyday Church: Gospel Communities on Mission* (Wheaton, IL: Crossway, 2012), 10.

hide her sin (4:17), but Jesus identified and exposed her true identity (4:17–18). This woman, despite her relationships with six different men—five marriages and one live-in boyfriend—had a desperately thirsty soul.

Jesus identified with this woman. He knew her sin, he knew her temptations, and he knew that her greatest need would be met in finding life in him. His identifying is not done in a condemning manner but one that is full of grace and love. Jesus was able to identify with the woman at the well, with you and me, and with our students because he became one of us, identifying with our humanity in every way, yet without sin. The writer of Hebrews captured this beautifully:

> Therefore He had to be made like His brothers in every respect, so that He might become a merciful and faithful high priest in the service of God, to make propitiation for the sins of the people. For because He Himself has suffered when tempted, He is able to help those who are being tempted. (2:17–18)

Just as Jesus identified the sin in the life of the woman at the well, we are called to identify the sin in the lives of the young people in our ministries. Week after week we interact with students who forsake the *"living waters"* in Christ for *"broken cisterns that can hold no water"* (Jer. 2:13). These broken cisterns reveal themselves in a myriad of ways—from pornography to eating disorders to drunkenness. While those behaviors are incredibly destructive, our students do not need condemnation but identification. Identifying and exposing sin in the lives of our students is messy, arduous, and uncomfortable, but necessary for the hearts and souls of those who are in desperate need of salvation in Christ.

As we identify sin, brokenness, and idolatry in the lives of our young people, we are able to point them to their daily need for Jesus. An essential part of making disciples is understanding our own ongoing need for Jesus, living moment by moment in faith in the Savior and in repentance for our lack of faith. As Jonathan Dodson noted, "In our everyday failures, we have every opportunity to turn to Jesus for grace and forgiveness. . . . A gospel-centered disciple rejects the pursuit of perfection and embraces the gift of repentance. In short, a gospel-centered disciple is a repenting disciple."[12] Discipling young people begins with initiation and engaging with them relationally, and moves toward identifying with who they are—pointing out sin and idolatry, and calling them to trust Jesus in every way. Discipling, however, doesn't and can't stop there. We must also show them how the gospel invades every part of their beings—from their identities to their relationships . . . and everything in between.

Youth leaders, your commitment to discipleship begins with the *initiation* of relationships with young people; this must be done carefully, lovingly, and intentionally. Discipleship continues with *identification*, as you begin to carefully and biblically point—in truth—to sin, brokenness, need, and hurt, which can only be fully and eternally addressed through repentance of sin and faith in Jesus Christ.

Now, the final step.

Invade

Despite the woman's attempts to take the focus off her sin, Jesus pointed her right back to her need. The Samaritan woman's whole life had been built on the externals: how she looked, what she did, with whom she was sexually active, and where she worshiped. Jesus wasn't concerned with what was on the outside; his concern was for her heart (Mark 7:14–15).

Jesus knew what this woman needed, and it was not another man or a mountaintop worship experience. What she needed was her life to be invaded by the living God.

Like this woman, many of our students are focused on the externals of life and will deflect the attention away from their sin. Jesus, however, is calling them to more. Are we following his lead and pointing them to more? Jesus was consistently inviting his followers

---

[12] Dodson, *Gospel-Centered Discipleship*, 83, 85.

to a deeper and fuller relationship with him. He pushed them to continue learning and growing as his disciples. Mike Breen put it this way: Jesus was "inviting his followers into a relationship with him while also initiating a direct challenge to behaviors he knew were either wrong or unhealthy. He drew his disciples closer, loved them, but also gave them the opportunity to accept the responsibilities of discipleship."[13]

Our students will remain in pursuit of momentary pleasures to cope with their sin through their moralism, sexuality, body image, self-righteousness, vanity, status, and many other things until the gospel of grace invades their lives. The Samaritan woman remained dead in her sin until Jesus invaded her life with what she truly needed—living water—and she went from an outcast in the community to a neighborhood evangelist (4:29; 4:39). In short, she "believed" in Jesus, giving herself fully to him in faith. Everything changed as she became a true disciple.

In our ministries we constantly come into contact with the woman at the well—the sinner, the student living in bondage to sin, guilt, and shame. Whether internally or externally, this person feels alone, hopeless, and bound to personal sin. Such a person needs faithful youth leaders who will lead him or her to Jesus and point to the Bible . . . not simply to a program or an event. While we cannot penetrate the heart of the student, we are called as God's laborers to communicate the sinfulness of sin and the love and saving power of the gospel. For relational ministry to be effective and to truly disciple an individual, we cannot neglect confronting sin, while providing the hope for the redemption that is found in Jesus. With the power and truth of the gospel, Jesus invaded the lives of each person he met. We are called to do the same.

In your discipleship, initiate relationships with students. Identify, gently and truthfully, the ways that other pursuits lead them away from Jesus. Finally, invade lives with the powerful truth of

---

[13] Breen, *Building A Discipleship Culture*, 17.

the biblical gospel. Declare the beauty of the salvation that is only found through loving, trusting, and following the Savior who died for sin and then rose again to grant eternal life to all who will follow him!

The Priorities of Discipleship

As we initiate, identify, and invade the lives of young people, we should constantly be evaluating their spiritual needs. The "end goal" of any youth ministry should be that the students know Jesus and are growing in Jesus. Unfortunately, our focus can become programs rather than people and, before we realize it, we've become program sustainers rather than disciple makers. The games, camps, retreats, and the like are all of value, but in the midst of the programs and craziness of youth ministry, we cannot neglect a greater understanding of where the students are spiritually.

As we initiate, identify, and invade the lives of young people, we should be asking ourselves: Are our students growing as disciples of Jesus? Are we providing avenues within our church and youth ministries to promote discipleship?

Over the years, I have come to the realization that simple is better in youth ministry. As we disciple the students in our ministries, we must understand where they are spiritually, provide a biblical framework to connect with them relationally, and design programs to meet their spiritual needs. Through that process, what undergirds everything in our ministries is the Bible. God's Word provides the infrastructure to teach and grow disciples. Teach the Bible; simple is better!

A simple, yet helpful, biblical framework for discipleship in youth ministry is to engage relationally and program thoughtfully with these three priorities in mind: the love of Jesus, the love of others, and the love of mission. In other words, as you disciple and lead young people, are they growing in their love for Jesus? Are they gaining an understanding of why they need other Christians, the body of Christ, around them? Finally, are they grasping the biblical value in going out serving and making disciples in their schools and beyond?

It should go without saying (but I'll say it anyway!) that the Bible will inform what it looks like for our students to love Jesus, love others, and love mission. This framework for discipleship must be formed and shaped by the clear teaching of God's Word. So, biblically, how can we preach and teach those three areas in all that we do in discipleship in youth ministry?

Love of Jesus

The first priority of discipleship is the love of Jesus. As students engage in our programs and as we initiate with them relationally, is it evident that they love Jesus and know Jesus loves them? Discipleship begins with Jesus. It seems simple, but it is so easy to depart from a Christ-centered purpose in discipleship! As Dietrich Bonhoeffer noted, "Jesus summons men to follow him not as a teacher or a pattern of the good life, but as the Christ, the Son of God. . . . There is no road to faith or discipleship, no other road—only obedience to the call of Jesus."[14] Relationally and programmatically we must be pointing students to Jesus—not to a program or a personality but to the only One who provides salvation, hope, and restoration to all of life.

Within our large group meetings we have the opportunity to disciple students and show them the necessity of knowing and following Christ. We should use those opportunities to paint a vivid picture of Jesus's undeniable love for them and his desire that they would follow him in all of life. As they gain a greater understanding of Jesus's love for them, they will grow in their love for and service of him. This is primary and essential in the discipleship of the students in our ministries. We must lead them to Jesus's love for them and their love for Jesus. True discipleship begins and ends with God's Son—the Savior and King of the entire world.

---

[14] Dietrich Bonhoeffer, *The Cost of Discipleship* (New York: Touchstone, 1995), 58.

Love of Others

The second priority of discipleship is the love of others. We should be teaching and modeling the necessity for our students to be involved in the church, the youth ministry, and in the lives of other believers. Through our relationships with students and our programming, are we communicating the value and necessity to be in small community with other Christians? Prayer groups, small groups, and discipleship groups are invaluable to the growth of our students through their years involved in our ministries; these will enhance and strengthen our commitments to Christ-centered discipleship.

The Lord often uses community to challenge us, grow us, and help us to find delight in glorifying him. God meets with his people "in those groups within the body of Christ in which the commitment to the kingdom of God and one another is of the highest priority. In the first church, committed life in community wasn't optional; it was normative."[15] Effective discipleship in the context of youth ministry will show students that growing in love for others is essential.

Love of Mission

Finally, we must focus our discipleship on the love of mission. As the students in our ministries are following Jesus and connecting with other believers, are they growing in their love of mission—the outward-facing service of others with the word of the gospel and with gospel-motivated love? The love for mission should not be viewed only through the lens of an early mission trip, whether stateside or abroad, but rather we should be shepherding our students to see their schools, athletic fields, and workplaces as mission fields. We need to be leading our students in such a way that, as Christians, they will "have relational integrity when they are integrated into the relational life of the city and when their faith is integrated into all parts of their lives."[16]

Whether in the suburbs or the "city," what is important is that

---

[15] Sine, *Taking Discipleship Seriously*, 47.
[16] Tim Keller, *Center Church: Doing Balanced, Gospel-Centered Ministry in Your City* (Grand Rapids, MI: Zondervan, 2012), 284.

we are showing, challenging, and biblically shaping our students so that their faith in Jesus involves all of life. It is here when disciples begin to make disciples, and when what we've displayed and communicated to them begins to be displayed and communicated in their everyday contexts. Living and loving life on mission is, as Tim Chester and Steve Timmis noted, "about living ordinary life with gospel intentionality. It is about doing what we already do with other people and with a commitment to speak of Jesus, whether to encourage believers or evangelize unbelievers."[17]

As we disciple students according to God's Word, then, we allow the Bible to shape more and more their love for Jesus, their love for others, and their love for being daily "on mission" for the sake of the gospel. May we be practicing what we preach as we disciple students toward these ends!

Looking Forward

The life-giving gospel of Jesus Christ is the beginning, middle, and end of discipleship. Those who follow Jesus are called to make him known—to make disciples who repent of sin and follow him wholeheartedly as well.

It is always about Jesus—the Savior and King who calls disciples to follow him with radical commitment and heartfelt worship. David Platt puts it this way: "Somewhere along the way, amid varying cultural tides and popular church trends, it seems that we have minimized Jesus' summons to total abandonment."[18] Student ministries have the market cornered, so to speak, on relational ministry and understanding the culture, but the youth pastor cannot be swayed by ministry fads and movements at the expense of the gospel and calling students to a radical commitment to Jesus. He must be central, for he is the Savior who gave all, and the King who demands all!

Brothers and sisters, will you recommit yourselves to disciple-

---

[17] Chester and Timmis, *Everyday Church*, 143.
[18] David Platt, *Follow Me: A Call to Die. A Call to Live.* (Carol Stream, IL: Tyndale, 2013), 3.

ship as your primary goal and calling in youth ministry? To this end, will you seek to actively *initiate* relationships with students, *identify* sin and idolatry in their lives, and joyfully *invade* their hearts and minds with the biblical gospel of Jesus? Then, will you invite them to walk with you on a path of discipleship—growing in love for *Jesus*, love for *others*, and love for *mission*? If you will, I am confident that you will see God's hand of blessing on your gospel ministry, as you joyfully call young people to follow the only true King and Savior.

More on . . . Discipleship

Dietrich Bonhoeffer, *The Cost of Discipleship* (1937).

Jonathan Dodson, *Gospel-Centered Discipleship* (Crossway, 2012).

David Platt, *Follow Me: A Call to Die. A Call to Live* (Tyndale, 2013).

Tom Sine, *Taking Discipleship Seriously: A Radical Biblical Approach* (Judson, 1985).

3

The Impact of Expounding God's Word

Expositional Teaching in Youth Ministry

Eric McKiddie

As a senior in high school I preached the first sermon of my life, nervously, to my youth group from Colossians 1. Jittery from drinking a Dr. Pepper for dinner and eager to get the thing over with, I plowed through my message. It wasn't a good sermon. I have the cassette tape recording in my parents' attic to prove it.

So when I was asked to preach to our junior high ministry a few months later, I wanted to improve. I developed a catchier outline around a clever topic, filtering in Bible verses along the way. It was a massive step forward.

Or so I thought.

A few years later, a girl a couple grades below me mentioned that first lesson and said it had influenced her. No one ever remarked on my "clever" lesson. That moment convinced me that expounding God's Word impacts people most—far more than human cleverness, humor, and creativity.

The pressure to entertain and to be relevant weighs on everyone who teaches the Bible to teenagers. It crushed me, and I was only two sermons in. Many youth pastors sacrifice Scripture for jokes or anecdotes, assuming that teenagers could never see the relevance of the Bible.

While fun is an indispensable part of youth ministry, your main task is to convince your students, week after week, why they need Jesus and to show how the gospel profoundly affects every area of life. Even gym class!

How do you teach God's Word like *that*? Why *must* you teach like that? And how do you dig into God's Word without emptying the seats of your youth meeting?

The answer to these questions, I believe, resides in the method of expositional teaching.

The Characteristics of Expositional Teaching

Expositional preaching has three main characteristics.

First, the sermon text is a single passage from Scripture, rather than various verses throughout the Bible. This could be a paragraph from a New Testament epistle, a narrative from a historical book, a psalm, etc. Expositional preaching seeks to *expose* what is in a single passage of the Bible.

Second, the theme of the expositional sermon is derived from the main point of the passage. This places two tasks on the youth pastor: (1) responsibly interpreting the passage, and (2) communicating that interpretation clearly and simply to your students. The goal is to proclaim what the biblical author intended to say to God's people *back then* in a contextualized, applicable way to God's people *today*.

Third, expositional teaching proceeds through an entire book of the Bible, from beginning to end, passage by passage. This enables you to teach each lesson in its proper biblical context, and to show how each individual passage supports the overarching theme of the entire book.

It's easier to generate your own sermon outline, mentioning a verse here and a verse there. But such teaching is rarely faithful to the original intent of the biblical author, and a diet of quick glances at Bible verses stunts spiritual growth. Expositional teaching allows teens to dive deep into the waters of God's Word, rather than skipping like a rock across the surface.

What would this look like in your youth ministry? Maybe four sermons on "God's Grace for Your Enemies" from Jonah, eight sermons on "The Joy of Suffering for the Gospel" from Philippians, or a semester on "Eternal Life through Believing in Jesus" from the Gospel of John. Each passage of each book will show your students the riches of the Bible and the innumerable ways it affects how we live.

Successful Youth Ministry Is God's Word at Work in Your Students' Lives

Youth pastors are prone to rely on programs, activities, and a killer worship band to make their ministry successful. On the other hand, youth pastors who don't have the facilities or budget to pull off a ministry like that can feel incapable of impacting teens for the kingdom. But a slick youth program is no substitute for a youth pastor who unapologetically teaches the Bible. God primarily does his work among those in his church (that includes the youth at your church!) through the preached Word. Consider the following verses:

- "So shall my word be that goes out from my mouth; it shall not return to me empty; but it shall accomplish that which I purpose, and shall succeed in the thing for which I sent it" (Isa. 55:10–11). Preaching the Bible guarantees that God will accomplish his purpose for your youth ministry. His Word is the key to youth ministry "success."

- "Our gospel came to you not only in word, but also in power and in the Holy Spirit and with full conviction. . . . You received the word in much affliction, with the joy of the Holy Spirit" (1 Thess. 1:5–6). Teenagers in whom God is at work do not cringe at a gospel-centered sermon from the Bible. Rather, they receive it with power and joy, even if it causes them to suffer.

- "When you received the word of God, which you heard from us, you accepted it not as the word of men but as what it really is, the word of God, *which is at work* in you believers" (1 Thess. 2:13). The Word of God continues to do its work in students' hearts when they go home from church, when they graduate, and even when you move on to another role in ministry. It's living and active (Heb. 4:12).

As you can see from these passages, the Scriptures resoundingly emphasize the priority of preaching the Word so that God may reveal himself and work in us. This is just as true with teens as it is with adults.

What results might your youth group experience due to your expositional teaching?

One result is that your students will learn how to study the Bible on their own. As you model how to interpret it by teaching through single passages, students will become acquainted with the Bible in the format in which they read it: chapters and books, not sound bites. Not only will this encourage them to do devotions, it will electrify their devotions, because they will know how to actually get something out of it.

Another result is that the students in your ministry will develop a biblical worldview as they become exposed to thorough teaching of God's Word. Comprehending how all the Bible's little messages fit together into its overall message will orient them to a system of thinking that is biblical. Thus they will not merely know that sin is wrong; they will understand *why* it is wrong. Armed with a biblical worldview, they will more effectively engage the culture and share the gospel.

Also, your students will become better prepared to serve others. Paul connects the teaching roles of the church with equipping the saints to do ministry (Eph. 4:11–12). Making the Word central in your teaching will help students discover their gifts and use them to serve within your youth group and the church as a whole.

PRACTICAL CONSIDERATIONS FOR EXPOSITIONAL PREACHING

Seven Steps for Preparing a Biblical Exposition for Youth

Having covered what expository preaching is and why it is important, let's now consider how to do it. The sermon preparation process I will describe can be compared to an hourglass: the first, second, and seventh step each take up the bulk of your time, while the middle four steps comprise a narrow—but all-important—transition between the beginning and the end. (But unlike an hourglass, it will take you more than sixty minutes to get from the top to the bottom.)

Step 1: Interpret the Passage, Just You and Your Bible

Pray for Illumination

Ask God to show you, by his Spirit, the meaning the passage had in its original context and its significance for both you and your students today (Ps. 119:18; 1 Cor. 2:10–16).

Familiarize Yourself with Your Passage

Read and reread the text. Look for repeated words and phrases, thought development, and emphasized ideas. Explore the context of the passage. How does it relate to the passage before and after? How does it relate to the message of the book as a whole? Do word studies on key words and phrases.

Write an Initial Outline of Your Passage

Outlining your passage reveals how each part fits together and how those parts support the theme of the passage as a whole.

Think of your passage like our solar system, with its sun, planets, and moons. The "sun" of your passage is its theme. The "planets" are the two to five main points that directly revolve around the theme. The subpoints are the "moons" that, though they certainly revolve around the theme (sun), more closely revolve around the main points (planets).

Don't underestimate the outlining step of the interpretation process. The biblical authors didn't merely rely on words to communicate their point. They also intentionally structured the individual passages and entire books to help bring their point home. As you outline the passage, its theme will emerge and you will begin to grasp the passage as a whole.

By the end of step 1 you will have an elementary understanding of your passage and will be ready to dig more deeply into it. Now is the time to turn to resources that will help you understand the passage more.

Step 2: Continue to Interpret the Passage Using Commentaries and Other Resources

Former seminary students will recall professors requiring them to exhaust every page of every book that anyone wrote on the passage they studied. But if we take that approach as youth ministers, we will have no time to disciple, train, or just have fun with our students. Therefore our goal should be to hit the most helpful books. What are those books?

Consult Two or Three Good Commentaries

I recommend that you use one or two technical commentaries and an additional devotional commentary. Technical commentaries plumb the depths of the text verse by verse, summarizing the ways it has been interpreted and arguing for one of those positions. Devotional commentaries (which are often nothing more than published expositional sermons) bring out the heart of the passage and will help you apply it. For the top commentaries on any book of the Bible, visit bestcommentaries.com.

Consult Biblical and Theological Dictionaries

Dictionaries contain articles on various topics relating to the Bible and theology, and go more in depth in those topics than a commentary. Look up concepts contained in your passage, or use the Scripture index in the back to find each place your passage is mentioned.

Consult Biblical Theologies

Biblical theologies explore how all the pieces of the Bible fit together into a coherent whole. They will help you see how your passage relates to the rest of Scripture. Like dictionaries, you can use the Scripture index in the back to look up where your sermon text is mentioned.

Consult Study Bibles

Many study Bibles, such as Crossway's *ESV Study Bible* (several different versions of this are available now), can also be reliable and helpful resources during this step of your preparation. Be careful not to lean too heavily on the explanatory comments; use them like conversation partners as you continue to work hard to plumb the depths of the passage you are preparing to teach.

Step 3: Determine the Fallen Condition Focus of the Passage

The "Fallen Condition Focus" (FCF) is the specific way your text addresses living in a sin-broken world. Bryan Chapell defines it this way, "The FCF is the mutual human condition that contemporary believers share with those to or for whom the text was written that requires the grace of the passage."[1] In other words, the FCF is the

---

[1] Bryan Chapell, *Christ-Centered Preaching* (Grand Rapids, MI: Baker Academic, 1994, 2005), 42.

spiritual problem raised by your sermon text that only the gospel can solve. This guards us from preaching moralistic, do better, try harder sermons. We can't fix our sin issues ourselves; we need God to do that in us, through the power of the gospel.

The FCF, more than cutting-edge videos or pop culture illustrations, demonstrates the Bible's relevance. What could be more relevant than addressing fundamental spiritual needs? Someone might object, "But my teens don't care about their spiritual needs!" In that situation, we must remember—and trust—passages like Isaiah 55 and 1 Thessalonians 1. Pray for the Spirit to use the Word he inspired to make them care. But for your students who *do* desire to grow in godliness and experience God's grace in their lives, the FCF functions like a mirror to their souls (James 1:22–25), leading them to repent of sin and receive the blessing of obedience.

How do you spot an FCF in your passage? Generally speaking, there are five types:

1. **Sin and sinfulness.** Ways we disobey God and thus need salvation through Jesus.
2. **Schemes.** How Satan targets us, for example through temptation and false teaching.
3. **Suffering.** Aspects of this world that reveal its brokenness, such as cancer, natural disasters, or abuse.
4. **Sadness.** Reminders that this world is not heaven, like death or unmet desires.
5. **Slip-ups.** Not sins necessarily but mistakes that expose our weaknesses. Common examples for students are not making the team, failing a test, or saying something stupid within earshot of the girl they like.

Step 4: Find the Gospel Solution in Your Passage That Counters the FCF

The good news is that, besides revealing our fallenness, each biblical passage also reveals God's grace through the gospel. The gospel is like a diamond. Every passage of the Bible contains a facet of the gospel that sparkles in a unique way. Our job as preachers is not only to point to the whole diamond of the gospel but also to the facets of the gospel in our sermon text.

Considering the fact that most of your students probably confess Jesus as Lord, it might sound weird to think about preaching the gospel in every sermon. If they have already believed the gospel, shouldn't we move on to new things? Yet Paul writes, "So I am eager to preach the gospel to you also who are in Rome. For I am not ashamed of the gospel, for it is the power of God for salvation to everyone who believes, to the Jew first and also to the Greek" (Rom. 1:15–16). You are probably used to hearing verse 16 in regard to evangelism. But Paul writes it in the context of preaching the gospel *to the Christians* who were in Rome! Christians never outgrow their need for the gospel. Rather, spiritual growth happens as we experience more of the grace that the gospel offers.

What does it look like to preach the gospel in a way that resolves the FCF of a passage? Here are some examples.

- In Ephesians 2:1–10, the FCF is that we are born dead in our sins (2:1), and the gospel solution is that we are made alive together in Christ (2:5).
- In Isaiah 40:27–31, the FCF is our tendency to accuse God of abandoning us during trials (40:27), and the gospel solution is to experience strength in waiting on God to act in his timing (40:31). The fact that God acted for Jesus on Easter Sunday after forsaking him on Good Friday assures us that, if we have trusted in Jesus, God will do the same for us.
- In 1 Thessalonians 4:13–18, the FCF is the grief we experience when another Christian whom we love passes away (4:13), and the gospel solution is to hope in the return of Jesus (4:14–18). Given how often our students lose godly grandparents, no youth pastor can afford to avoid this message.

Notice how *right in each passage* there is a fallen condition to address—sin, suffering, and sadness—*and* a gospel solution to that condition. We are unable to solve our sin problem on our own. But God imparts his grace to us through his Word and by his Spirit so that we are transformed all the more into the image of Christ.

Step 5: Develop Your Key Applications

There are two guidelines to keep in mind when you develop your applications.

First, determine what life change your particular passage requires. Don't make the mistake of preaching a true application from the wrong text (youth pastors are notorious for making "read your Bible and pray" the takeaway from every sermon). What sins are specifically pointed out in *this* passage? How are we called to obey God in *this* text? What promises in *this* passage would radically change how we live, if we really believed them?

Second, develop applications that flow from the gospel solution of the passage. This helps your students see their obedience to God as a response to his love and grace for them, not a way to make God pleased with them. Otherwise, you risk leading your ministry toward legalism. Grace, not rules, changes hearts. But a changed heart regards God's rules with loving delight (Ps. 119:47).

Step 6: Turn Your Lesson Preparation
into a Unified Sermon Outline

After step five, the bulk of your research is complete. Assemble your study into a skeleton outline of your sermon. Write out your FCF and the theme for your sermon. Align the sections of each main point with the structure of the passage, and phrase them in a way that relates them clearly to your theme (possibly sharing a key word or phrase). As you formulate your outline, keep your gospel solution in mind, so that the whole sermon drives toward it, making God's work in Christ the climax of your message.

Now is also the time to cut content out and deliberately arrange what you keep. In light of the burden of *this* sermon, what did you learn from your commentaries that you should leave out? How can you organize your material so that it comes across with maximum effect?

Step 7: Compose Your Sermon

A gospel-centered, expository sermon should have four main sections.

Section 1: Introduction

The goal of your introduction is to grip your students with the FCF and the theme of your sermon. An illustration of the FCF from real life will accomplish this. Acclimate the teens to the passage itself by pointing out the verses from which you derived the FCF and theme.

Section 2: Body (Your Main Points)

Whether you have two, three, or five main points, each one generally contains three parts. First, give an *explanation* of the verses of the passage that correspond to the main point, and convey why what the verses say matters today. Second, tell an *illustration* that connects the Bible to the world that today's students inhabit. Pull from teenager-friendly places like music lyrics, TV shows, movies, and sports, but don't neglect passages from novels, interesting science facts, and accounts from your own life experience. Third, provide a call to *application*, showing how our hearts should be affected by the passage and giving examples of how to live it out.

Section 3: Preach the Gospel

Until now you've been analyzing the passage and pleading with your students to respond to it. But they ultimately don't have the power to change on their own. Show them the gospel solution to the FCF in order to show how God—through what he has done in Jesus, by his Spirit—promises to work in them the change that he calls us to.

Section 4: Conclusion

Summarize your message, but try not to re-preach it. Provide a few final exhortations in light of everything you've said, especially in light of the gospel solution. Send your students home trusting God's work in them, rather than their work for God.

Looking Forward

I hope this chapter has been helpful, as I've sought to offer very practical and step-by-step instructions for forming and building an expository message for young people. Let me leave you with one of the most encouraging verses in Scripture for those learning to teach and preach God's Word. It comes from 1 Timothy 4:15; Paul tells the young pastor:

> Practice these things, immerse yourself in them, so that all may see your progress.

Here's the point: You may not turn into a great teacher overnight. But, with a steady and consistent commitment to teaching the Bible in an expository way to your students, they should see your progress! And, by God's grace, you will see the joyful progress in your own heart and life as God uses his Word in powerful ways through your teaching.

More on . . . Expositional Teaching

I've only had space to touch on the absolute basics of expositional preaching. But if I've whetted your appetite to learn more, here are four books I suggest you read as you continue to grow as an expositional preacher.

Daniel Akin, David L. Allen, and Ned L. Mathews, *Text-Driven Preaching: God's Word at the Heart of Every Sermon* (B&H, 2010).

Bryan Chapell, *Christ-Centered Preaching: Redeeming the Expository Sermon* (Baker Academic, 1994, 2005).

David Helm, *Expositional Preaching: How We Speak God's Word Today* (Crossway, 2014).

David Murray, *How Sermons Work: A Very Helpful Book for Those Who Prepare Sermons* (EP, 2011).

4

Emulating God's Heart

Building Relationships in Youth Ministry

Liz Edrington

I am convinced I've been given the absolute best chapter to write in this book. I get to write about relationships. I mean, really? Is there any topic more connected to the heart of God and the heart of Christianity? As I sit in a fantastic little coffee shop, pondering the myriad ways I've seen and known Jesus through relationships in my life, I can't help but smile. What a banquet! As I will not necessarily have the chance to sit and have coffee with you, I hope you will get to know me just a bit through my words; for I am convinced that relationship (even if only through the page) is the vehicle for healing just as it is the vehicle for wounding. It is the space for some of the most important things that happen in ministry; it is the place we share in the mystery of who is love incarnate.

Theology in Relationship: The Invitation to Live in the Tension of Mystery

You'll notice that Scripture and theology are peppered throughout this chapter. This is intentional and serves as a picture of the way we can interact organically with our students in Bible-founded, gospel-centered, theologically rich ways. The following three sections (on the Trinity and creation, on the incarnation, and on the word of the cross) are designed to set the stage for exploring the way we relate to God, others, and ourselves.

Welcome to the Party: On the Trinity and Creation

If God had not a communicative, spreading goodness, he would never have created the world. The Father, Son, and Holy Ghost were happy in themselves, and enjoyed one another before the world was. Apart from the fact that God delights to communicate and spread his goodness, there had never been a creation or redemption.[1]

One of the most beautiful elements of Christianity is the dynamic of the Trinity. We find the scent of the Trinity beginning in Genesis with the exclamation of God to the Godhead, "Let us make man in *our* image, after *our* likeness" (Gen. 1:26). And we see that Jesus is the radiance of God's glory and the exact representation of his being in many places in Scripture (John 17:20–26; 2 Cor. 4:4; Col. 2:9; Heb. 1:3).

As three distinct persons in one God, the Trinity expresses relationship in its most foundational form—love flows from one person to the next to the next and spills out over creation. God isn't needy; he is abundant. He didn't make the world and humans to keep himself company or puff up his self-esteem; he is not lacking in anything. It is in his very nature to *share*, to *give*, and to *welcome*. He *delights* in communicating and spreading his goodness.

In *Mere Christianity*, C. S. Lewis paints a picture of the Trinity

---

[1] Richard Sibbes, "The Successful Seeker," in *Works of Richard Sibbes*, ed. Alexander B. Grosart (Edinburgh: Banner of Truth, 1983), 4:113.

as "a dynamic, pulsating activity, a life, almost a kind of drama. Almost, if you will not think me irreverent, a kind of dance."[2] The analogy of being invited to a dance might not quite tickle your fancy, but what about being invited to a fantastic banquet where the Father, Son, and Spirit are enjoying themselves?

Or for me, I imagine being invited to a pickup game of soccer where three of the most fantastic players I've ever seen are out on the pitch having the time of their lives. They each have different gifts and roles (much as do the persons of the Trinity), but they are one God, sharing in one brilliant game that they are continually inviting me into . . . my favorite game in the world.

I love the soccer metaphor (although it is far from perfect), because when I play, I experience what Eric Liddell was talking about in the movie, *Chariots of Fire*, when he says, "And when I run, I feel [God's] pleasure." For me, it's not actually the running, it's being caught up in the dance, in the rhythm of the game—of players moving to get open, of the dynamics of the ball heading toward me, of considering teammates' strengths and weaknesses to send them the best ball, of the ebb and flow of possessing the ball while looking for an opportunity to shoot or create a play. It is a taste of the Trinity and I *experience* what Richard Sibbes is talking about: I *feel* God's delight in communicating and spreading his goodness. It is intensely *personal*.

In Living Color: On the Incarnation

It is a profound wonder that God decided to enter time and space to meet us right where we stood—right in our sin and our messy attempts to love. John 1:1–18 gives voice to the mystery of Jesus's existence before time as the Word as well as his humble, flesh-enrobed entrance into history. In him, 100 percent humanity and 100 percent deity exist together in a way that *always* invites others to *be known and loved*. The incarnation offers us a constant reminder that he is Immanuel, *God with us*. Not only did he humbly

---

[2] C. S. Lewis, *Mere Christianity* (New York: HarperOne, 1952), 175.

choose to put on skin, walk among us, and live the life of a human, experiencing all of the physical, emotional, and spiritual highs and lows that we experience; but his whole life pointed to, and culminated in, an act (on the cross) that shouted of how "for us" he is.

It is essential for us to consider the way Jesus, the God-man, treats humans as spiritual beings, as embodied souls (1 Cor. 6:19–20), and not as brains on sticks or as data consumers. We can see this in his complex and mysterious parables in response to folks' questions in the Bible. We also see it displayed when he responds with emotion to people instead of with words. Lazarus's death in John 11:1–36 is a poignant example. Here, Jesus does not offer a scriptural explanation for death or jump to quoting Scripture about redemption. He sits in the tension of Mary's loss *with* her, and he grieves *with* her. He meets Martha in her emotional need with his presence and tears. In the same way, we want to minister to our students as whole human beings, considering not only their minds, but their hearts, bodies, and spirits as well. In our information age, we are living more and more into the identity foisted upon us as data consumers, so your willingness to minister to the heart of your students will reflect the heart of Jesus in more significant ways than you may know.

That Sweet Sound: On the Word of the Cross

The word of the cross can be summed up by monumental words spoken by Jesus in John 19:30: "It is finished." Sin no longer has the final say over our lives, leading to the death we deserve; we are made alive through the grace of God's gift offered us via the cross (Eph. 2:1–5). Our need to fulfill the law for salvation is finished, being fulfilled by Jesus on our behalf. With and in Christ, we are dead to striving after our salvation, and we are free to follow our God who has purchased us with Jesus's blood. We are justified by no means of our own and made friends with God instead of enemies (Rom. 5:10) through the atoning sacrifice of Jesus Christ.

Knowing (and continuing to recognize) our own need for the message of the cross allows us to receive the grace and truth we can then offer to our students. Romans 3:1–31 reminds us that we are fundamentally the same as our students: we are broken image bearers of God who desperately need Jesus's redemption. Even as leaders, we always need the reminder that "it is finished," and that our identity is rooted in him. We are forgiven, we are justified, and we have been brought from death to life. At no point (this side of the Jordan) will we *not* need to seek, listen for, and trust the Holy Spirit to lead us. It can be tempting for us to see ourselves as a messiah for our kids, and parents often minimize our role as merely that of being a "good example and role model." But I implore you to walk into student relationships with humility, as a sinner in need of grace. The cross tells us that we are in need, the same as our kids.

PRACTICAL CONSIDERATIONS FOR BUILDING RELATIONSHIPS IN YOUTH MINISTRY

Thinking in Threes

As a fan of the Trinity, I like to think of things in threes, and it has really helped me to break down and consider relationship in three categories: relationship with God, relationship with self, and relationship with others. Beginning with God, we know that he does not merely give us *information* about himself; he gives us *his very self* in the form of Jesus. Whether or not you subscribe to some version of "incarnational ministry," you cannot deny that the act of God humbling himself—taking the form of a man to rescue his creation from sin and death—is important to consider when we think about how to do youth ministry. He deals with us up close, not impersonally from afar.

Relationship with God: Prioritize Your Relationship with Jesus

The *where* of where God's grace and truth intersect *your own* life will play an essential role in discovering what you have to offer your students in individual relationships. Where have you known his pursuit of you, *his* renaming of you as beloved son or daughter, *his* invitation to repentance and reconciliation?

Taking time to pray, worship, and read the Bible is absolutely vital in ministry; we are made to be fed by the Word of God who is the Bread of Life (John 6:35). Scripture reminds us who we are, who God is, and who the kids are to whom we are ministering. We cannot offer what we ourselves do not have. We are made to have our proverbial cup filled up by the Lord and then to pour it out into our ministries.

Relationship with Self

Nearly all the wisdom we possess, that is to say, true and sound wisdom, consists in two parts: the knowledge of God and of ourselves. . . . For quite clearly, the mighty gifts with which we are endowed are hardly from ourselves; indeed our very being is nothing but subsistence in the one God. . . . Accordingly, the knowledge of ourselves not only arouses us to seek God, but also as it were, leads us by the hand to him.[3]

Know Your Own Story

God has written (and is writing) your story with unique twists and turns, dreams and disappointments that shout of his bigger story, the kingdom of God, that we read about in Scripture. We need to know our own story deeply because connecting with our students cannot occur unless it is a part of the conversation. How has Jesus been strength in your weakness? How has he redeemed bits of your brokenness and used it to reveal himself? How has God drawn you to himself? The answers to these questions are an integral part of your story, and they will be great gifts to the students you work with.

We live in the tension of the broken realities that sin has wrought in our lives and the world alongside the hope of Jesus's

---

[3] John Calvin, *Institutes of the Christian Religion*, ed. John T. McNeill, trans. Ford Lewis Battles (Philadelphia: Westminster, 1960), 35–37.

redemption. We live in an era where all won't be right until "Aslan comes in sight" again (or in the fancy theological term: *inaugurated eschatology*).[4] This means we are free to be honest and even confused with God, when we experience things that bring us unfathomable pain and suffering, such as a broken heart, the loss of a loved one, or unexpected hard times.

God *already* knows us at that depth of anger, disappointment, or confusion, and he loves us there (1 John 3:16–20). Acknowledging, facing, and processing our past allows us to truthfully operate in relationship with Jesus, others, and ourselves. Without knowing your story (your past), you miss out on the intricate ways God has been working to draw you to himself, to *see* and *feel* your need for him, to *know* him in darkness, and to *long* for him to return.

Value Community—Love Begets Love

Take a second and think of someone who had a profound impact on your faith—perhaps someone who really made you believe that you mattered, made you feel known, or made you believe that God's love was real at a difficult point in your life. This is someone who the Lord used to "fill your cup." How did this person reflect Jesus's love to you?

I can remember the sweet surprise of walking up to my locker freshman year of high school to find it decked out with a colorful poster full of encouraging words and quotes. The culprit? Katie, my former middle school Young Life leader and current "big sister" on the field hockey team. She was a picture of intentionality, using her senior year to write me kind notes with Bible verses on them, check in with me in the halls, and remind me that I had something valuable to contribute to the team. She shared the love, hope, and purpose she'd come to know through the gospel with me in our relationship.

In addition to mentor-like relationships, our personal/peer relationships have a significant trickle-down (or trickle-over?) effect in

---

[4] C. S. Lewis, *The Lion, the Witch and the Wardrobe* (New York: HarperCollins, 1950), 80.

our ministries. For this reason, it is so important to live vulnerably and share Scriptures in our own spiritual communities. This is a part of the way love begets love; mutual support and encouragement fills us up and becomes a picture of the church for our students.

Seriously, People: Soul Care and Boundaries

We have little to offer and give in ministry if we are spiritually dried up and running on fumes. The demands of ministry can seem unending, and there will always be more we can do. Learning our emotional and relational limits, and learning to say no, is absolutely crucial. I have often seen, heard of, and partaken in the over-scheduled, hamster-wheel comparative ministry conversations that *casually* drop in details about how much we've done or have to do. Without being aware, we are searching for some sort of validation and justification for the madness that is wreaking havoc in our families and peer relationships. Let us repent and seek to care for ourselves in the way God invites and calls us to. Sabbath is no less than a command, my friends, and given for our good, because making time to delight in God in the way he uniquely created us to connect with him (e.g., soccer) is absolutely essential.

Relationship with Students

Know Your Students, Volunteers, and Families

We, as youth ministers, get the incredible honor of entering into the worlds of our students, volunteers, and families, just as God graciously entered into our own world. We get to find out what they like, what they hope for, what they dream of, what they wonder about, where they hurt, and where they come from. We get to meet them on their territory and love them where they are. Football games, glorious middle school band concerts, plays, family dinners, and coffee shops become the landscape of ministry.

Our God-given curiosity is one of our greatest assets. Let your curiosity formulate open-ended questions (who, what, why, when, where, and how) and invitations for those around you to *be known*.

Empathy is another word for incarnational love, for gracious presence sharing. Empathy meets someone where they are emotionally and says, "I'm with you. Tell me more," whereas sympathy says, "I pity you. Wouldn't want to be you." Empathy joins whereas sympathy separates and distances. God relates to people in grace and truth (John 1:14), and empathy is the grace side of that equation, which allows the truths we share to be heard.

Values Are More Caught Than Taught

In chapter 1, Cameron Cole talked about how what you do in ministry reflects what you believe. Another way we can understand this is through the concepts of extrinsic (taught) and intrinsic (caught) learning. Our kids learn not only from the outward, spoken teaching we offer them, but also from the unspoken (and sometimes unconscious) beliefs that are displayed in our actions.

I will never forget the first time Ashley joined me in our soup kitchen one Tuesday. She was uncomfortable and unsure of how to interact with our guests. And as I walked around, enjoying catching up with my street friends and asking them about their various interests, I noticed that she began to relax. Over the next couple of weeks, I watched as she began to join that community in a similar way over time; she delighted in her time with these folks as I did. She watched me bestow the dignity upon them that others have bestowed upon me, and she intrinsically learned about relationships and the church. She watched me experience blessing through and from my street friends, and she gradually experienced the same.

Your Vulnerability Opens the Door for Their Vulnerability

I personally connect most with and remember teaching when someone has shared a little of their own story. When I sense someone's humanity and genuineness, I am able to remember more of what they are teaching. There is great humility in sharing vulnerably, and it has a profound impact on the listeners. Jesus-in-the-abstract becomes Jesus-in-the-flesh to students as you offer them the truth of what it is like to wrestle with faith and doubt, suffering and hope.

We want to be wise in how vulnerable we choose to be with our students, as we do not want to invite them to take responsibility for anything unfinished in our lives or for pain we have experienced. Here are a couple of helpful hints for considering what and how to share:

1. It is good to hold off sharing a particular story if we sense that we are still in the process of being "unraveled" over it versus considering it from the other side where we've seen a bit of redemption.
2. We want to make sure we have already shared and processed our story with someone in our mentor or peer community.
3. If it is a story of our sin, we want to ask if our story includes repentance and/or grief over what we are sharing, or does it celebrate the sin/make it look appealing?

We Have Something to Learn from Our Students and Families

Questions, ideas, and perspectives of kids can be amazing. Even Jesus talks about having faith like a child (Mark 10:13–16). We have something to learn from everyone in God's creation—whether it is about hope, evil, redemption, wisdom, strength, perseverance, or something else. Look for the lessons your students teach *you* through their questions and honesty. Look for the impact they have on *your* life as you seek to impact their lives for the sake of the kingdom. This idea helps us to approach others humbly and in an open posture, versus setting ourselves up to be the-powerful-one-with-all-the-answers (which, we aren't, by the way).

The Holy Spirit Is Our Mediator and Advocate (1 Tim. 2:5)

Remember, this isn't all about you and what you do or do not know, or what you do or do not have to offer; Jesus *is* your ability to relate to your kids. I have often been guilty of falling into the trap of believing that I need to have all of the answers to care for my students well. But I am *convinced* that the Holy Spirit *in* me is the most important piece of the equation in a relationship with a student. It can be much easier to rely on our own knowledge (or fret over our lack thereof) versus *trusting God* to show up and provide what a student needs in a moment (which may actually be more about listening than talking anyhow).

Ministry can be absolutely exhausting and unraveling. And it is a total privilege as well. Let us continually seek and rely on the Holy Spirit for guidance in our lessons, our retreat plans, our mission trips, our discipleship of volunteers, our calendars, and our relationships with parents. He alone can sustain us and fill us (John 14:26; Rom. 8:26).

Practice Remembering

We can take one from the Israelites' book: We are people who constantly forget who God is, who we are, and who the others were and are who have impacted our lives. We forget our origins, we forget our true identity, and we forget what we are made for. We get comfortable in Egypt—in our enslavement to worshiping and seeking lesser things—because it is familiar.

We need help remembering, and one of the sweetest things we can do in community is to share the stories of God's work in our lives together. Crafting stories together is powerful. I want to invite you to set aside time at the end of retreats, mission trips, small group seasons, and community gatherings to mark your time as a group—in whatever way that looks. Memory sharing, testimonies, highs and lows, and thank-yous are great for wrapping up a significant time.

Enjoying the Sacred in the Ordinary

We need to be involved in the daily lives of our kids, and we need to involve them in ours. Kids are curious about what it looks like to follow Jesus day in and day out (the sacred in the ordinary), so we want to let them into that reality. Especially in the current social media world, we might be tempted to make more of our lives than the actual experience, and we might be tempted to make everything we do in our ministries "special." Yet we, and our stories, are *enough* because in and with Jesus, *we* are enough (Col. 2:9–10). Sharing in the ordinary with your students is a crucial aspect of ministry; we believe in a God who uses ordinary means to express and share himself. He came as a human; he used bread and wine to teach about and share himself.

It can be tempting to make our testimonies or stories more dramatic for greater appeal, but when we embellish, we are robbing our students of the glorious work of the Holy Spirit through ordinary means. We create a vision of Christianity as mountaintop experiences and miracles in lieu of the mysterious, rough-and-tumble adventure that it truly is.

Looking Forward

It was the regularity of being invited into the lives of my Young Life leaders throughout middle and high school that created a vision of the church for me; there was a grounded stability in these wonderfully kind, generous folks welcoming me week by week into their homes and faith. This is not to discount the miraculous and awe-inspiring ways God works in our lives as well. But let us consider how to offer both the ordinary and the extraordinary means through which God works in our lives. Let us always return to Jesus—who he is, what he did, and the hope of his return—to inform the ways we relate to God, our students, and ourselves in our ministries.

More on . . . Relationships

Francis Chan, *Multiply: Disciples Making Disciples* (Cook, 2012).

Matt Chandler, *Explicit Gospel* (Crossway, 2012).

David Helm, *One-to-One Bible Reading: A Simple Guide for Every Christian* (Matthias, 2011).

5

Community Based on the Gospel

Building Community in Youth Ministry

Mark Howard

Being in community is part of what it means to be human. We all interact with others at some level. For youth, community takes many shapes. Sometimes youth engage in communities that are superficial and tend to be self-promoting, like Facebook, Twitter, and Instagram. They participate in performance-based and competitive communities like school, sports, band, orchestra, and drama. Some communities are forced upon the youth, like family, school, and church. Youth also participate in self-selecting communities such as cliques and clubs.

For those ministering to youth, it's important to be aware of the many communities that influence youth on a daily basis, as well as how the dynamics of these communities impact community within any youth group. Intentionality is required if we seek to form a community based on the gospel of Jesus Christ and *not* based on superficiality, performance, competition, self-selection, or selfishness. This chapter will help to clarify the nature of Christian community, specifically as it relates to youth ministry, with a view toward discerning practical means for fostering such a community among youth.

The Theological Basis for Christian Community
Christian Community Is in Christ Alone
It may be obvious, but it's worth stating at the outset: by definition, there is no Christian community without Christ and his life, death, resurrection, and ascension. Scripture tells us that Jesus is the cornerstone of the church (Eph. 2:19–21). He is the Head of the church (Col. 1:18). Jesus is the One in whom all things hold together (Col. 1:17). As the German theologian Dietrich Bonhoeffer wrote in his exploration of Christian community:

> Christianity means community through Jesus Christ and in Jesus Christ. No Christian community is more or less than this. Whether it be a brief, single encounter or the daily fellowship of years, Christian community is only this. We belong to one another only through and in Jesus Christ.[1]

Without Jesus, a youth group has no foundation, no head, and no glue to hold it together as uniquely Christian, for it is only in our union with Jesus in his cross and resurrection that we find our communion with one another.

Christian Community and Our Adoption in Christ
It is here that Paul's metaphor of adoption is instructive. In his letter to the church in Galatia, Paul writes:

---

[1] Dietrich Bonhoeffer, *Life Together: The Classic Exploration of Christian Community* (New York: Harper & Row, 1954), 21.

> When the fullness of time had come, God sent forth his Son, born of woman, born under the law, to redeem those who were under the law so that we might receive adoption as sons. And because you are sons, God has sent the Spirit of his Son into our hearts, crying, "Abba! Father!" So you are no longer a slave, but a son, and if a son, then an heir through God. (Gal. 4:4–7)

Paul talks about adoption here to underscore the truth that God did not redeem us in Christ merely to be his subjects, but to be his *family*. According to this passage, God sends the Spirit not primarily to make us obedient bond servants, but to enable us to be joyful children who feel free to cry out to God. And he does this because of his gracious love, as Paul notes in Ephesians: "In love [God] predestined us for adoption as sons through Jesus Christ, according to the purpose of his will, to the praise of his glorious grace, with which he has blessed us in the Beloved" (Eph. 1:4–6).

John continues this theme in his first letter: "See what kind of love the Father has given to us, that we should be called children of God; *and so we are*" (1 John 3:1). He goes on to write, "Beloved, we are God's children *now*" (v. 2). Our status as fellow children of God is a present reality, for as Paul wrote to the church in Ephesus, "You are no longer strangers and aliens, but you are fellow citizens with the saints and members of the household of God" (Eph. 2:19). Therefore, again quoting Bonhoeffer:

> Christian brotherhood is not an ideal which we must realize; it is rather a reality created by God in Christ in which we may participate. The more clearly we learn to recognize that the ground and strength and promise of all our fellowship is in Jesus Christ alone, the more serenely shall we think of our fellowship and pray and hope for it.[2]

It's this gracious nature of our adoption in Christ into the family of God that awakens us to five facets of Christian community.

---

[2] Ibid., 30.

1. **It is God-initiated.** As our adoptive parent, God is the instigator behind all Christian community. Unlike social clubs and cliques, Christian community is not allowed to be self-selecting.

2. **It is grace-based.** Given the gracious nature of our adoption, our participation in Christian community is not contingent on our worthiness. Unlike school, sports teams, musical groups, and drama clubs, Christian community is not to be based on performance or competitive.

3. **It is love-driven.** Our inclusion within the Christian community comes through the boundless and self-giving love of the Father in Christ by the Spirit. Therefore, unlike Facebook, Twitter, and Instagram, Christian community does not seek superficiality or self-promotion.

4. **It is church-focused.** Because our adoption is into the full family of God, Christian community firmly locates the more narrow goal of community within the youth group, within the larger reality of community within the wider church body. In Christ we become family with the entire church that transcends space and time, not just friends within a youth group. This reality should shift our primary goal from making the youth good "church kids" during their adolescence, to cultivating engaged and maturing members of the corporate church body. Thus, fostering community within the youth group cannot be an entirely separate endeavor from cultivating the youth's participation within the wider church. Our failure on this point may be one of the primary reasons why so many youth walk away from church life once they go to college: they never really felt a part of the corporate church community in the first place; they only felt a part of the youth group.

5. **It is inherently diverse.** The reality of our adoption into the household of God leads us to anticipate diversity in the family of God. It is full of people who are "other" than us, though we share a common identity as humans who are deeply loved and called by God.

Christian Community Reflects the Triune Nature of God

God's triune nature gives insight into the nature of Christian community. Not only does the doctrine of the Trinity teach that community is inherent within the Godhead (three in one), it also reminds us that Christian community is both a participation in and a reflection of God's triune nature. Jesus himself prays that we may be one even as he is one with the Father: "I in them and you in me, that they may become perfectly one" (John 17:23).

We notice, too, in Trinitarian theology, that the community of the Godhead is a unity in diversity, not a unity in uniformity. As the Athanasian Creed states, "The true Christian faith is this, that we worship one God in Trinity and Trinity in Unity, neither confusing the Persons nor dividing the substance." As ministers to youth, we should resist community that only comes through uniformity, and instead seek to cultivate a diverse community formed around the gospel.

PRACTICAL CONSIDERATIONS FOR BUILDING COMMUNITY IN YOUTH MINISTRY

Pray for Unity

So how do we work to more fully realize the unity we already have in Christ in our youth groups? Thankfully, as we read in Galatians 4, the Spirit is already at work teaching us to cry out together, "Abba! Father!" as members of the one household of God. Therefore, if Christian community is a gift from God through our adoption into his family, then the first thing we should do is turn to God in prayer. If we want to experience true Christian community in our youth groups, then we must regularly pray for a fuller realization of that unity in our midst.

Be Christ Centered

Since Christian community is found in Christ alone, ensure your youth group is focused on the means that God has established to point us to Jesus: Scripture, prayer, and the sacraments while in fellowship with other Christians. Youth leaders are often pushed and persuaded to put themselves, fun, games, moralism, numbers, or something else at the center of the youth group's identity, but it's unrealistic to think that Christian community will be manifest if something or someone other than Jesus is at the center of our fellowship.

Be Cross Focused

Since the reality of our Christian community comes through the cross of Jesus, it makes sense that a fuller realization of that community is found in the way of the cross. Jesus said, "If anyone would come after me, let him deny himself and take up his cross daily and follow me" (Luke 9:23). So also Paul writes in his letter to the church at Philippi:

> Do nothing from selfish ambition or conceit, but in humility count others more significant than yourselves. Let each of you look not only to his own interests, but also to the interests of others. Have this mind among yourselves, which is yours in Christ Jesus, who, though he was in the form of God, did not count equality with God a thing to be grasped, but emptied himself, by taking the form of a servant, being born in the likeness of men. And being found in human form, he humbled himself by becoming obedient to the point of death, even death on a cross. (Phil. 2:3–8)

The cross of Jesus is not only to be the subject of our teaching and preaching; it is to be the guide for our interactions with one another. As youth ministers, we should be working and praying for a proclivity toward humility, service, sacrifice, and concern for others in our life and in the lives of our youth. This is particularly important as we train up youth leaders. Actively seek to provide opportunities for the youth to serve one another, other church members, the local neighborhood, and the wider world.

Teach, Preach, and Model That We Are Family

In our teaching and preaching, it is easy to focus on the individual aspects of salvation and neglect the corporate aspects of what God has done for us in Christ. As you proclaim the gospel, make sure to regularly remind the youth and your leadership team that God's love has not only saved them and united them to Jesus, but has also made them God's family and united them to one another. One good way to go about this is to cultivate traditions that strengthen the bond of your youth group family. Traditions have a way of initiating new members into a group while reinforcing the leadership potential in the more seasoned participants. Annual events, retreats, activities, and youth leadership teams can all work toward this end.

It's also important to prepare the youth for changes in family dynamics that will inevitably occur in the youth group. Whenever a class graduates and a new class enters in, the dynamics of the youth group are bound to shift as the makeup of the group changes. Tragedy is another game changer for many youth groups. If a friend commits suicide, a student dies, a tornado hits, or a shooting takes place, the impact will ripple through the youth group. It's here that being Christ centered and cross focused really makes a difference. Christ is the only foundation that can ground the group through the shifting sands of changing circumstances. Also, the cross provides the only lens through which pain and suffering find true meaning and healing. This is where the hope of resurrection gives the strength to view trials as opportunities to love one another as God's family.

Teach and Preach a Unity That Is Found in Jesus, Not in Uniformity

Unless we are actively cultivating a community that embraces diversity within our youth groups and churches, we will continue to mirror the uniformity or disunity that defines so many of our world's communities.

Be Aware

As leaders, we need to be aware of cliques that are forming and cultural trends that dominate the group so that we can continually reorient the group around Christ and his cross. Some influential kids in a youth group I led for many years were fans of the TV series, *Dr. Who*. Before long, it felt like you had to watch *Dr. Who* to be a true member of the youth group. It wasn't a good dynamic, as it slowly sidelined the kids who didn't like *Dr. Who* or weren't allowed to watch the show.

Be Thoughtful

So also, we need to be careful not to plan events and programs that inherently exclude members of the group or inadvertently develop a community of shame. I learned this early on in my days as a youth leader. I had chosen a popular movie to watch and discuss as a part of our Sunday evening program. The goal was to help the students see gospel truths at work in popular film and use those insights as inroads into meaningful conversations with their friends. I had good intentions, but my plan backfired. The youth group was comprised of sixth- through twelfth-grade kids, some of whom came from families that didn't let their twelve-year-old kids watch PG-13 movies. So they couldn't come. What was worse, though, was the fifteen-year-old kid whose parents wouldn't let him watch PG-13 movies. Not only was he unable to participate, but he felt ashamed of his parents and was embarrassed to answer kids as they asked him why he couldn't participate. Rather than fostering unity, this event became a divisive wedge that could have fragmented the youth group if not reconciled.

Be Intentional

Where I currently live, many of the churches are comprised of a narrow demographic. What does it look like to pursue unity in diversity in a predominantly uniform setting? First, it means learning to see and appreciate the diversity that already is present in terms of race, economic status, personality, and interests (more on that later). Secondly, it means being intentional about exposing the youth to people who are different than the dominant demographic of the local congregation. This can be done by bringing in guest speakers, participating in multichurch gatherings, or having the youth visit different churches. Though not their main purpose, mission trips and service events also help to expose youth groups to new segments of the local or global Christian community.

Be Appreciative

Every kid is different. As you spend time with the youth, spend time learning what makes them unique. As you do so, find ways to celebrate the diversity God has already placed in your youth group. Encourage the youth to go to each other's plays, karate demonstrations, math competitions, concerts, sports games, and other activities. Find ways to encourage their individuality and help the youth envision how they can use those skills and interests to serve the church. We all have a part to play in the family of God (that's the heart of Paul's teaching in Romans 11 and 1 Corinthians 11).

Encourage the Youth to Participate in the Full Life of the Local Church

Though youth group can play an important role in the spiritual development of the youth, corporate worship and congregational life need to remain the primary focus of the youth's participation in the church. After all, youth in Christ are not adopted into the youth group but into the full family of God. Therefore, our aim is to cultivate maturing disciples of Jesus who are committed to the family of God, not simply good youth group participants. This means that as youth pastors, we need to be intentional about equipping the youth to more fully participate in and appreciate corporate worship.

A good way to do this is to view the programs of the wider

church (e.g., choir, praise team, women's ministry, men's ministries, missions team, etc.) as ways for the youth to get involved in their church. Not only does this reduce the amount of programs you need to plan and pay for, but it has the added benefit of helping the youth get to know the adult members of the church. This is particularly important since you can't be all things to all youth—especially given their diversity. Encourage and help the youth network with others in the church who can effectively minister to their unique needs. It's freeing to realize that you don't have to do it all. Community within the youth group is not and should not be separate from community with the local body of Christ.

Remember the Family Business: Reconciliation

It would be unrealistic to write on community among youth without talking about ministering amid disunity and fractured community. All families have conflict, and the church family this side of Jesus's return is no exception. Sin inherently frustrates relationships and fosters disunity. Thankfully the good news of the gospel is that the unity we have in Christ is full of new life born of forgiveness, repentance, and reconciliation. Paul writes:

> Therefore, if anyone is in Christ, he is a new creation. The old has passed away; behold, the new has come. All this is from God, who through Christ reconciled us to himself and gave us the ministry of reconciliation; that is, in Christ God was reconciling the world to himself, not counting their trespasses against them, and entrusting to us the message of reconciliation. Therefore, we are ambassadors for Christ, God making his appeal through us. (2 Cor. 5:17–20)

As a Christian community with Christ at the center and focused on the cross, giving and receiving forgiveness, practicing repentance, and pursuing reconciliation remain essential to experiencing the unity we already have in Christ. This means that we have to learn to be peacemakers, actively pursuing conflict resolution and teaching the youth to resolve conflict biblically. It also means that a Christian community is always looking to reach out to those outside the community to bring them into the family of God.

Looking Forward

In the end, Christian community is meant to be dynamic and life giving, for it is found in a living God who remains on the move in our midst. Ours is a redeeming God whose love continues to draw into his family those being saved. Praise God for the part we get to play in proclaiming the gospel of Jesus Christ! Youth ministers, commit yourselves to teaching about, pursuing, and building gospel-centered community in your ministries. Celebrate unity in Christ in the midst of diverse people and diverse gifts. Teach about the importance of this kind of community, reminding your students regularly that the church of Jesus Christ has the potential for bringing together all kinds of people around one glorious Savior who offers a gracious salvation. Then, enjoy the richness of the togetherness in the gospel that begins to flourish, for the glory of God.

More on . . . Community

Dietrich Bonhoeffer, *Life Together* (1939). A short theological treatise considering the nature of Christian community.

Trevor J. Burke, *Adopted into God's Family: Exploring a Pauline Metaphor* (InterVarsity Press, 2006). A biblical theology exploring Paul's use of the adoption metaphor.

Ken Sande, *The Peacemaker: A Biblical Guide to Resolving Personal Conflict* (Baker, 1991, 1997, 2004). This book is an extremely helpful and practical guide on biblical principles for reconciliation. Ken Sande also has a student edition and youth curriculum that are useful tools to provide concrete skills in conflict resolution for youth (more information at www.peacemaker.net).

6

Building a Foundation with the Parents

Partnering with Parents in Youth Ministry

Mike McGarry

Youth ministry is temporary because adolescence is temporary. That might come as a tough pill to swallow for some youth workers, but we all know it is true. This does not mean youth ministry is insignificant, neither does it overlook the long-term impact a faithful youth ministry can have on a young Christian's life. Teenagers are only teens for a few years, and then they graduate from the youth ministry. If youth workers have not sought to intentionally help students build their faith in both the local church and in the home, then they simply have not fulfilled their calling in an enduring way.

Unfortunately, conversations about the relationship between youth ministry and parents can sometimes lead to poor assumptions, or even worse, harsh accusations. As the growing family-integrated church movement continues to cast blame on churches for "age segregation" and undermining parental authority, youth workers are often tempted to discount many valid critiques because of the unfair stereotypes and extreme conclusions.[1] Similarly, those who reject the validity of youth ministry in favor of family discipleship seem to elevate the family above the church in a way that reflects a low view of the church. Instead of falling into a debate mind-set, we must embrace a vision whereby the church and parents coevangelize and codisciple their teenagers.

As youth workers, it is essential to remember that every student has a family he or she returns to when leaving a youth group. We can talk about how we view ourselves as a support to the family, but too often we are guilty of paying only lip service to this notion. Ministry to parents must be more than a good idea. Mark Cannister describes the importance of ministry to parents by emphasizing, "Partnering with parents means helping them recognize, understand, and embrace the significant depth of their influence and the numerous modes in which they can contribute to their teenager's development of a sustainable faith."[2] Because parents are the primary faith influencers of their children,[3] the cost of investment into parent ministry should not be seen (negatively) as time that could have been spent with youth, but as a long-term investment in their family.

Biblical Foundations for Family Ministry

Family Discipleship in Community Context (Deut. 6:4–9)

Moses wanted to ensure that the coming generations would know Israel's history and be faithful to the Lord. In the midst of God's deliverance of Israel, it defies comprehension that parents would

---

[1] For more on the family-integrated church movement see: Timothy Paul Jones, ed., *Perspectives on Family Ministry: Three Views* (Nashville: B&H Academic, 2009).

[2] Mark Cannister, *Teenagers Matter: Making Student Ministry a Priority in the Church*, Youth, Family, and Culture (Grand Rapids, MI: Baker Academic, 2013), 180.

[3] Christian Smith and Melina Lundquist Denton, *Soul Searching: The Religious and Spiritual Lives of American Teenagers* (New York: Oxford University Press, 2009), 56. Steve Wright and Chris Graves cite multiple nonreligious studies affirming the primacy of parental influence in: Steve Wright, *reThink* (Wake Forest, NC: InQuest Ministries, 2007), 81–82.

neglect teaching their children who the Lord was and what he had done for Israel. And yet, only two generations after leaving Egypt we read, "There arose another generation after them [the generation of Joshua] who did not know the LORD or the work that he had done for Israel" (Judg. 2:10).

This command to parents was squarely set within the broader context of renewing Israel's covenant with the Lord. More specifically, this particular command follows the repetition of the Ten Commandments in Deuteronomy 5. If their children were unfaithful to the Lord, Moses knew the Lord would destroy them (Deut. 6:15; 7:1–3). It was of utmost importance that parents were faithful in teaching their children to fear the Lord and to keep his commandments. The verbs "teach" and "talk" (6:7) carry the force of commands to the parents to not merely tell their children about the Lord, but to deliberately structure their family life around worship so that the Lord's commands would be engraved on their children's hearts.[4]

In the midst of the parental duty to disciple their children, it must be noted that these commands were given to parents within the entire community ("Hear, O Israel . . ."). Today's concept of the nuclear family (mom, dad, and children living as a family unit, separate from extended family) is very different from the biblical family.[5] Most families lived together as a clan, and if they did not share a family home together, they generally lived in extremely close proximity to each other.[6] This is important to remember because of the broader implications for intergenerational discipleship. The father and mother were certainly given chief responsibility to disciple their children, but it was also understood to be a community project.

The Christian message is not one of mere law keeping, but is a proclamation of adoption and grace by faith. Accordingly, the

---

[4] As Piel verbs, their verb form serves to intensify the action which is commanded.

[5] The *Oxford English Dictionary* dates the earliest usage of "nuclear family" to 1924.

[6] Stanley E. Porter, "Family in the Epistles," in *Family in the Bible: Exploring Customs, Culture, and Context*, ed. Richard S. Hess, M. Daniel Carroll R. (Grand Rapids, MI: Baker Academic, 2003), 152–53.

church and Christian parents teach their children the commands of God in order to present their children with the gospel of grace, poured out through Christ Jesus the Lord through his death for sins and resurrection from the dead. Parents should view themselves as their children's "first pastors," while simultaneously inviting other church family members to codisciple their children.

When ministering to a group of "church kids," it can be easy to forget that we must never passively assume our children will confess Christ and serve him. Every person needs to be evangelized before they can be discipled, and although most pastors and parents would heartily agree with this, it is a reality that is frequently ignored. Children only become children of God through the gospel, as they repent of sin and trust Christ personally, not through family lineage.

The Family Reflects the Church (Eph. 5:22–6:4)

In Ephesians 5:22–6:4 Paul is not simply outlining family structure but explaining that the family reflects God's fatherly love. The family reflects the gospel to children. This is why so many of us can see clear parallels in our relationship with God as our heavenly Father and our relationship with our earthly father. The family inherently teaches something about who God is, how he loves us, and the power of redeeming grace when we have sinned.

We are born into a family; we are adopted into the church. The family is an earthly metaphor for the eternal family of God we know as the church. Adoption and membership in the church is not genetic but only comes through saving faith in the gospel. Some discussions regarding the "dropout rate" among churched teens sometimes forget that a "churched teen" may never have been converted. Thus, the dropout rate may accurately track church attendance but not teens' standing before God.

When parents view their spiritual duty as being fulfilled by bringing their children to church, Christian formation simply will not happen at home. We should not be surprised when lukewarm parents produce lukewarm kids. Faithful reflection of the gospel will only happen when parents themselves have been transformed by the grace of God. The formation of a Christian worldview in the home requires both formal and informal instruction, which many well-intentioned parents feel unprepared and inadequate to provide.[7] This reflects the importance of the church's calling to disciple parents in order that they may disciple their families. Although youth workers may not lead the adult discipleship ministries, they provide key support and encouragement to the parents (especially for those who feel inadequate).

Youth Ministry Feeds into the Mission of the Church

Youth ministry cannot be a bridge unless it is equipping students to grow deep roots in the local church. When teenagers have never experienced worship, prayer, discipleship, or fellowship within the church at large, why would we expect them to suddenly be receptive to full involvement in the church when they graduate?

It is so natural to focus a youth ministry on the teenagers. Instead, youth ministry must always remember its context (the church) and build a bridge into the homes where the youth live (the family). When a teenager has a sound faith, which is firmly rooted in both the church and the home, he or she will be exponentially more likely to continue in the faith long after high school. Jay Strother issues a wise reminder when he states, "God designed church and household to serve as the two faces of one intentional process of proclaiming and practicing the gospel."[8]

Additionally, as the family of God, the church provides a surrogate family for those who do not have a Christian family. We need to rally around the next generation and show teenagers what it looks like to follow Christ as a twentysomething, as a parent, as a grandmother, and as a widow. Each member of the local church

---

[7] Barna Research Group, *Parents Accept Responsibility for Their Child's Spiritual Development but Struggle with Effectiveness*, May 6, 2003 (accessed April 22, 2014), http://www.barna.org /barna-update/article/5-barna-update/120-parents-accept-responsibility-for-their-childs-spiritual -development-but-struggle-with-effectiveness.

[8] Jay Strother, "Making the Transition to Family-Equipping Ministry," in *Trained in the Fear of God: Family Ministry in Theological, Historical, and Practical Perspective*, ed. Randy Stinson and Timothy Paul Jones (Grand Rapids, MI: Kregel Academic, 2011), 255.

needs to be embraced as a family member with something valuable to invest in the next generation. If students never feel at home in "big church," and only know the confines of the youth room, then we should not be surprised when they do not get plugged into the church after graduation.

Youth Ministry Serves as a Bridge between the Church and Family

Youth ministry is temporary because adolescence is temporary. Once students graduate from high school they are no longer "ours" (as if we owned them to begin with!). Teenagers are entrusted to our care for a few short years. Youth ministry is an important arm of the local church where the church and parents have the wonderful opportunity to coevangelize and codisciple, with the desire that God would draw students to himself.

Bridges are important. You can't get over a river without one, but no one builds his home on a bridge. If a youth ministry is not consistently seeking to nourish a student's faith to grow deep roots in the local church, as well as at home, then the student's faith will naturally develop around the youth ministry. For this reason, a youth ministry must be intentional about positioning itself as the church's ministry to teenagers and their parents rather than simply being focused on the youth alone.

This means a church must not see ministry to teens as something delegated to the "youth leaders." Instead, the whole church should place a high value on intentionally welcoming the coming generations and encouraging them to meaningfully contribute to the life of the church. When this happens, the church's ministry to youth will extend well beyond the organized youth ministry. Likewise, when families in the church are consistently instructed to be their children's spiritual leaders, and are equipped to carry out that calling, the church may find itself filled with youth who desire to serve in both the youth ministry and beyond. The church's youth ministry should be the greatest advocate and resource to see both the church and the parents catch a vision for this deep partnership, especially when it ministers to the youth by looking beyond the youth alone.

Obstacles to Parent Ministry

Youth ministry has long placed a high value on ministry to parents, but most of us have failed to put this into practice for a number of reasons.

1. Most simply, it is really hard to do this consistently. Placing a high value on ministry to families requires much attention and effort, often with few immediate results. Ministry to parents must be consistent over the long haul, and that is a commitment that is not easily maintained over time.

2. The harsh reality is that many parents resist help. Many parents will be content to offload their children's spiritual development to the church. Others, especially non-Christian parents, simply will never see you as more than neutral: not a bad influence, but not a partner either. This is why those who attend parent meetings and workshops already see you as an ally in codiscipling their children, while those who really ought to attend do not.

3. Many youth workers seem to like teenagers more than they like adults, which obviously makes ministry to parents more difficult. Teenagers simply seem more approachable and less intimidating to youth workers than the teenager's parent. If this describes you, then you need to break out of this comfort zone and work on establishing relationships with parents, not just with their kids.

4. Through conversations with other youth workers, it seems that there is a myth that you cannot value families and be an evangelistic youth ministry at the same time. Unchurched teenagers need the church, not just a youth ministry. We must continue to seek and save the lost through the power of the gospel, which also has the potential to transform their entire family through the wonderful grace that is found in Jesus Christ.

5. Most pragmatically, some resist this bridge building because it simply is not cool and students want a "parent-free zone." While we should provide space for teens, we should also work to unite families rather than divide them. If attendance is king, this is not the ministry philosophy for you.[9] On the other hand, if you want to see students and their families bear lasting fruit, then I am convinced you must have an intentional commitment to affirm both the local church and the family.

PRACTICAL CONSIDERATIONS FOR PARTNERING WITH PARENTS

Bridge Building 101: Getting Started

Overcommunication Is Impossible

The most obvious foundation that must be laid with parents is clear and consistent communication. Parents should be well informed about the details of the youth ministry calendar and deadlines. Additionally, it would be wise to provide some way to communicate a summary of what has been taught in youth group meetings. When communication is lacking, relationships will rarely be established. Consistently reaching out to the parents will affirm to them that you see them as valuable partners. Setting up a blog or social media account for the youth ministry can be a wonderful way to share important information not only with the youth but also with the parents.

Get Parents Together

Hosting parent meetings is a continual source of frustration for many youth pastors. If these meetings have heavy agendas, you

---

[9] I do not believe you need to choose between attendance or families, as if they are mutually exclusive; but if your church highly prizes gaudy attendance then this will probably not be a good fit for your ministry.

should anticipate thin attendance! As alluded to above, many of the parents who attend are the ones already invested in family discipleship, while the parents who most need to attend these meetings will rarely come. In the past, I have gotten great feedback after hosting "Parent Potlucks," where each parent comes with a food to share and the parents simply eat together. You may be surprised how few parents of teenagers know each other well. This was a great way to gather the parents together twice each year for fellowship, to share a few strategic details about the youth ministry, and to ask them how my leadership team and I could bless and encourage them.

Make the Calendar Reflect the Value of "Family Time"

This philosophy of ministry issues a direct challenge to the "more equals better" mentality when it comes to programming. You must resist creating a ministry calendar that contradicts your emphasis on family discipleship. How can a family meaningfully spend time together if they are always separated at church and away from home for church events or programs? Do not be afraid to cancel youth group meetings when they fall on a holiday or just before or after a big ministry event, whether it is a youth ministry event or another significant event in your church. Your calendar has the potential to demonstrate or destroy the picture of your commitment to family discipleship and unity in the gospel.

Seek to create at least one opportunity this year where you can bless the families in your church through a program that will bring families together. Our ministry recently hosted a Family Feud night where families competed against each other, and students whose families either could not or would not come were "adopted" into a new family for the night. The students and parents both had a fun time together, while reinforcing the importance of the family. Sure, we could've had higher attendance if we hosted a high-energy game night (and those have their place too!), but we chose this program in order to give families a lasting memory together.

Be Your Church's Advocate for Families

You need to see yourself as an advocate for the youth and parents to other church leaders. Speak up to promote families during staff meetings, elder meetings, and whenever you have the opportunity to remind other ministry leaders of the importance of intentionally equipping parents to lead in family discipleship. Encourage your pastor to think about parents and youth in his sermon preparation. Although most of this equipping may not be through the youth ministry in particular, it is vitally important to your ministry to ensure it is happening. If your church is not equipping parents to evangelize and disciple their children, then you need to become the advocate for this activity. Without making accusations, inquire to ensure that current classes for parents are not simply focused on discipline or other "family basics," but strongly admonish those class leaders to be teaching parents how to lead family devotions and how to talk about faith with their children.

Be Patient!

As you get started, remember that bridges are not built in a day. They take time, and foundations must be poured carefully and given time to settle before adding more infrastructure. Think big; start small. This bridge building may have enormous ramifications, not only for your youth ministry, but also for your entire church and the families associated with your ministry. Communicate the biblical foundations for the ministry shift to the pastors and other church leaders, recruit a team to prayerfully discern what the bridge at your church will look like, and expect this transition to take three to five years.

Frequently Asked Questions

What about Unchurched Teenagers?

The church family becomes a "surrogate family" for students whose families are not Christian. I have personally seen previously unchurched students experience this as Christian families have naturally welcomed them in. I have seen other families start attending church because their teenager wanted to come. When Christian families catch a vision to invite unchurched teens to church, who then become honorary members of the family, Christian parents and children can partner together in reaching into young people's lives with the gospel.

If you and your church can reach out to the parents of unchurched students to become a resource and to cultivate trust, they may eventually realize that you are a potential partner rather than an adversary. Seek opportunities to bless and affirm their family, building bridges whereby unbelieving parents may be drawn into the life of the church.

Does This Mean "Youth Group" Is Wrong?

No, absolutely not. It is good and helpful to provide targeted, age-specific ministries to teenagers. Adolescence is a challenging and formative stage of life where students are no longer children, but they are not yet adults. It is important for teens to have a safe place in the church where they can experience Christian fellowship, ask hard questions, and open up the Scriptures with their peers and Christian adults who care about them. What I am saying *is* wrong is twofold: (1) neglecting the importance of ministry to the students' families and (2) failing to plug students into the broader life of the church (their faith family).

What about Unresponsive Parents?

Keep on pursuing them! Don't give up. There will always be some parents in the church who willfully or unwittingly neglect the calling to disciple their children, while others may hear it but do not think they are capable of fulfilling it. Do not let the parents who want you to be a spiritual babysitter discourage you. As new families are coming to Christ, they will need to be instructed that family discipleship is something they should be doing. Keep repeating this message and keep emphasizing the responsibility and honor of family discipleship. Who knows how many times it will take for certain parents to understand and faithfully obey?

Looking Forward

Youth ministers, we have a tremendous opportunity before us to partner with believing parents in the midst of our congregations and communities in the grand task of teaching and discipling their children as followers of Jesus Christ. This partnership is not easy; sometimes it will be messy and may even require much more work than simply operating in a different sphere from family life. But, it will be worth it. Let's give ourselves to intentional cooperation and unity with Christ-following moms and dads who welcome our help, support, and encouragement. We may even find ourselves ministering to them as much as to their kids!

More on . . . Partnering with Parents

Resources for Church Leaders

Mark Cannister, *Teenagers Matter: Making Student Ministry a Priority in the Church* (Baker Academic, 2013).

Reggie Joiner, *Think Orange: Imagine the Impact When Church and Family Collide* (Cook, 2009).

Paul Renfro, Brandon Shields, and Jay Strother, *Perspectives on Family Ministry: Three Views* (B&H Academic, 2009).

Randy Stinson and Timothy Paul Jones, *Trained in the Fear of God: Family Ministry in Theological, Historical, and Practical Perspective* (Kregel Academic, 2011).

Resources for Parents

Jason Helopoulos, *A Neglected Grace: Family Worship in the Christian Home* (Christian Focus, 2013).

Walt Mueller, *The Space Between: A Parent's Guide to Teenage Development* (Zondervan, 2009).

Paul David Tripp, *Age of Opportunity: A Biblical Guide to Parenting Teens* (P&R, 2001).

7

Gathering God's People

Generational Integration in Youth Ministry

Dave Wright

I sat nervously talking to the pastor of a church of more than five thousand members that he had planted from nothing. He was a confident man who carried himself like the CEO of a major corporation. I was a mere twenty-one-year-old, fresh out of college, interviewing to be the next youth director. Most of the interview was pleasant and I thought it was going well. Then, he hit me with the toughest question. "Why is it that I have thousands of people coming to worship here, and yet we can't seem to get young people to attend our services?"

My bonehead reply was something about not understanding why youth would not enjoy the excellent services offered. I was being truthful but naïve. The services were excellent. The music was the best you could find anywhere. The preaching was outstanding. The atmosphere was warm, welcoming, and exciting with so many people coming each week. Despite my naïve response and desire to flatter, I got the job as youth pastor.

It took me less than a year to figure out why young people did not attend corporate worship there. The reason had nothing to do with the fact that it was a traditional church. It was not about teenage rebellion, nor the lack of relevant music or worship style. The reason youth did not worship there was because they never had. From the earliest days of that church, everyone under eighteen attended Sunday school classes while adults attended worship services. The reason for offering Sunday school during the worship services was pragmatic. The church grew so fast that space was an issue, and simultaneous Sunday school was the solution.

A practical solution to a space issue led to a problem that is fairly common: a lack of integration between the generations.

What Scripture Teaches Us

The segregation of generations in worship is not seen in Scripture. This is a more recent development in the church. Scripture shows us examples of the people of God gathered for various acts of worship at which all ages are present. We need only look at a few biblical passages that specifically mention the presence of the younger generations to see that there is something of a norm here. Descriptions of the generations gathered for worship are not commands to that effect, however, so it is worth also looking at instances where the Lord directs his people to gather the generations in worship.

The reading of God's Word is an act of worship where we see all generations present in Joshua 8.

And afterward he read all the words of the law, the blessing and the curse, according to all that is written in the Book of the Law. There was not a word of all that Moses commanded that Joshua did not read before all the assembly of Israel, and the women, and the little ones, and the sojourners who lived among them. (Josh. 8:34–35)

Prayer and confession is an act of worship, and we see the generations gathered for that in Ezra 10.

While Ezra prayed and made confession, weeping and casting himself down before the house of God, a very great assembly of men, women, and children, gathered to him out of Israel, for the people wept bitterly. (Ezra 10:1)

In Acts 20:7–12 we see a gathering of God's people as Paul preached a rather lengthy sermon. A young male present, by the name of Eutychus, who was likely between the ages of seven and fourteen, drifted off to sleep during the sermon and fell out of a window. While the account is there in Acts to show the miracle performed, we also see who was present for Paul's preaching. Then we also see in Paul's letters to the Colossians and Ephesians instances where children are instructed to obey their parents (Col. 3:20; Eph. 4:12–13). As these were letters intended to be read aloud to congregations, we see nothing to suggest that the children were specially brought into the service to hear these words. Paul's words here are directed specifically to children that he expected to be sitting in the congregation. He's not speaking about them, but to them. The obvious implication is that children were present in worship. Exactly what ages were present is beyond speculation but the point is this: Worship in the early church included all generations.

For many years my study of the book of Nehemiah focused on his visionary leadership. When I got to the middle of the book, I stopped, because the wall was finished and the mission accomplished. I should have read further. In chapter 8 we see the generations gathered for the reading of the book of the Law of Moses. The vast crowd gathered to hear from God's Word included adults and nonadults. We don't know the specific age range, but the text tells us that men, women, and all who could understand were present.

When we read on, we see the celebration of the Feast of Booths. In Deuteronomy, God's people are instructed how to properly celebrate the feasts (Deut. 16:9–14). The Feast of Weeks and the Feast of Booths are specifically linked to a command to include the generations in the celebration. Exodus 12:24–27 provides instruction on the celebration of the Passover, in which children are to be included. In Joel 2:15–16, we see God calling his people to assemble to fast and consecrate themselves. This call to worship includes all generations. None are exempt.

In the Gospels, we see that Jesus lovingly accepted and even prioritized children and had a special heart for them (Matt. 18:10–14; Mark 10:13–16). He expressed a clear desire for children to follow him and obey him, giving strong warning to those who might lead them into sin (Matt. 18:5–6). In Jesus's world, children were the only category of preadults. Adolescence, as we know it today, did not exist. Thus we need to pay attention to how Jesus approached children in order to see his concern that they were taught well, in order to be able to understand his teaching and work.

In the book of Acts, we see several specific instances of families coming to faith and being baptized together. Even when Jesus calls his disciples to leave their families and follow him, we see evidence that some of their family members were following as well (Matt. 20:20–21; Mark 16:1). We also see admonishment for older believers to guide and instruct the younger (Titus 2). This is consistent with the commands to pass the faith from one generation to the next (Deuteronomy 6; Psalm 78).

The picture we get from Scripture consistently shows us intergenerational worship, rather than segregated worship. There is no evidence of the equivalent of youth church or even children's church in the Bible. The early church followed the Old Testament command for older generations to disciple the younger. This is done naturally when the church is intergenerational in nature, rather than segregated.

PRACTICAL CONSIDERATIONS FOR GENERATIONAL INTEGRATION IN YOUTH MINISTRY

Snapshots of Youth Ministry in the Church

While the pattern we see in Scripture of including the generations should be our norm, there are several different patterns that we see broadly in the church today. Perhaps a glance at three scenarios that I have witnessed firsthand will help clarify where your church is currently. The examples of youth ministry that we see in the church can be described as: segregated, associated, and integrated.

Segregated

The *segregated* youth ministry sees students relegated to the youth room whenever the church comes together. This might mean a youth service or Sunday school taking place during normal Sunday morning worship. When church-wide events are offered, the church is intentional about having a youth program. Often church leaders will insist on youth and children's programs being offered in order to provide something for everyone. The rationale given is that, because of this, the whole family is in church at the same time. Occasional family events might take place, but they are the exception and not the norm. Youth are given one Sunday each year to help lead the morning services, and adults are thereby reminded of the thriving ministry to students. The youth pastor in this scenario may not feel well connected to the whole staff. Likewise, students don't generally know how to relate to the church beyond youth group participation. This level of segregation is far more common in very large churches than in smaller ones.

Associated

The *associated* youth ministry is somewhat connected to the overall church body. Students are seen in worship with the congregation, but still remain mostly separated from the life of the church. A youth Sunday provides the one time that students participate in the worship service beyond sitting in pews or serving in token roles. The church also might have a youth choir. There are more likely to be church-wide events where there are not specific programs for teens. Some students will have relationships with adults other than youth leaders, simply because they are around the church members more often. However, most students' experience of church is limited to the youth group, as well as sitting in corporate worship on Sunday mornings.

Integrated

The *integrated* youth ministry sees students as an integral part of the congregation. They not only are seen on Sunday mornings in worship, but often take key roles in leading and serving. These roles might include choir or music team, ushering, reading Scripture, prayer ministry teams, running sound or video, and greeting. There might not be an annual youth Sunday because they are already involved in worship every week. Students are incorporated into church-wide events and have relationships with people of all generations. All ages serve side by side in the church with an integrated youth ministry. Youth groups and Bible studies still exist in this model, but are an addition to the experience of being part of the congregation. Students who enter the church through the youth group usually find themselves connecting to the whole congregation.

Only in the integrated scenario do we truly see all ages together as the body of Christ worshiping God, hearing the preaching of his Word, praying, learning from each other, sharing in Holy Communion, and enjoying fellowship. Students are not left wondering what the purpose of the church is because they experience the church of Acts 2:42–47. They learn that the church exists to glorify God and not simply to please them and meet their age-specific "needs." They experience the process it takes to "equip the saints for the work of ministry, for building up the body of Christ, until we all attain to the unity of the faith and of the knowledge of the Son of God, to mature manhood, to the measure of the stature of the fullness of Christ" (Eph. 4:12–13). This is an intergenerational context where students know people in every stage of life who are living out their faith in the midst of all kinds of challenges. This is the church, and students know how to engage with it.

An integrated youth ministry is able to provide students with a full experience of the body of Christ without eliminating the youth group entirely. Some would advocate for a radical integration where youth ministry does not exist. I don't believe the answer to segregation is the elimination of youth groups or other age-specific ministries. Rather, the church must minister to students by including them in all aspects of church life. The provision of a youth group is not a substitute for this but an additional means of discipleship and a place where they can minister to peers through Bible teaching, small groups, and vibrant fellowship.

Unintended Consequences

What are we telling students about the church when every time people gather at the church building, the youth have a separate program? What message do we convey when we give them one Sunday each year to participate in leading the service? Do we imagine they look forward to the day they will be grown up and can participate in "big" church? Have we considered that when that day arrives, they might not understand anything about it and simply walk away from it altogether? Or, will they search out a church that most resembles their youth group experience because it is less foreign to them? These are vital questions for the segregated ministry.

Several unintended consequences come when we limit the integration of our youth ministry into the life of the church. These consequences come in at least three areas: understanding, observing, and continuing in the gospel.

Understanding the Gospel

First, without integration, our students may develop a limited *understanding* of the gospel. The common approach of youth ministry is to address the issues facing students. In doing so, students can get the sense that Christianity is primarily a set of morals or a self-help process of becoming a better person. This perception stems from the struggle adolescents face in establishing their identity. When students also sit under biblical teaching delivered to all ages, they get a better sense of how the gospel shapes the whole life—at every stage.

Observing the Gospel

Second, our students may develop a view of how the gospel changes lives that is limited to the stage of life we call adolescence. They *observe* very little of how God is working in the lives of people of all ages unless they are relationally integrated into the life of the congregation. Younger generations learn as much from what they observe as they do from what we actually tell them. These two consequences create a very teencentric faith and create a challenge for students to relate to the rest of the church body.

Continuing in the Gospel

The third unintended consequence, which follows the first two, is the reality that young people will struggle *to continue* as part of the church in later years. When youth group is all they know of the Christian experience, the only place to turn after graduating is another youth group–like experience. There are a good many churches that have built on this consequence and created churches that look like youth ministries from recent decades. Yet those generally do not provide intergenerational relationships either, leaving the next generation of students to struggle with the first two consequences. We serve our students best when we integrate them into the life of the church, helping them to experience the church with all the generations.

We do teens a disservice when we segregate them from the life of the church. When we build youth ministries that do not engage students in the life of the congregation, a future of empty pews is the unintended consequence. Pew Research reports that twenty- to thirty-year-olds identify with Christianity at half the rate of their parents and a quarter of the rate of their grandparents.[1] These young adults were teens a decade or two ago, and many of them were active in church youth ministries. Many are asking what we can do to get them back into church. Maybe young adults are not actually leaving the church; they were never really there to begin with.

It is time that we engage students in the life of our congregations. Only then and there can we model and shape a biblical view of the church as we pass the faith from one generation to the next.

From Segregated to Integrated

We see in Scripture two realities that should shape our approach to youth ministry. One is that when God's people gather to worship, all the generations tend to be included. The other is that faith being passed from one generation to the next is the Lord's intention. The family is the primary place for this, but the assembly of believers is also part of the process. Through these we know that younger generations grow up understanding what it means to be in God's covenant community. If a church decides to take seriously the patterns and instructions seen in God's Word, then the task is to move from segregated or associated into a more integrated model of youth ministry. The process for doing this includes educating, including, and raising expectations.

Education

Students must be *educated* as to what the church is and how it functions. This is best when taught explicitly, as well as modeled. Adults need to learn about the challenges that teens face today in order to be able to support, nurture, and encourage them. In the church that has come to accept segregation, Scripture must be taught so

---

[1] Allison Pond, Gregory Smith, and Scott Clement, "Religion Among Millennials," *Pew Research Center*, February 17, 2010, http://www.pewforum.org/2010/02/17/religion-among-the-millenials.

that the whole congregation understands God's intentions as well as the benefits for all.

Inclusion

Intergenerational relationships occur when students are *included*. Not only do they witness the gospel at work in the lives of people at all stages of life, but Scripture commands that the older generations are meant to teach younger people how to be men and women of God. Studies have shown that where young people grow up with intergenerational relationships, they are far more likely to remain involved in the church for life.[2] Opportunities for intergenerational relationships need to be created and encouraged in the church.

Expectations

Finally, *expectations* must be raised about what youth are capable of doing in church. In order to integrate students into all aspects of the life of a congregation, the members must see the capabilities of youth. They must not be seen as the church of tomorrow but brought into the life of the church *today*. This is in part an education process, but it also takes time to demonstrate that students can participate meaningfully in the church.

Key Applications and Questions to Ask in Your Church and Youth Ministry Situation

Give Students Meaningful Roles in the Church

Are there meaningful roles for teens in your church on a regular basis? Do students read Scripture, participate in the worship team, lead prayers, greet, usher, or serve in any other ways in worship? Offering students such opportunities makes them feel as if they are a contributor in the church here and now. This feeling only enhances the chances that they will continue in such a role as they enter adulthood.

---

[2] Mark Kelly, "Research: Parents, Churches Can Help Teens Stay in Church," *Lifeway*, August 7, 2007, http://www.lifeway.com/article/lifeway-research-finds-parents-churches-can-help-teens-stay-in-church.

Engage Young People in Sermons

Do sermons effectively engage all generations? A sermon that can be understood on various levels, including illustrations that touch every generation, is far more effective for all ages. When a pastor makes sermon applications that address the situations of teenagers' lives, he communicates to the teens that they are a part of the larger body. He says that the leadership considers teenagers important members of the congregation. When a pastor *never* demonstrates how the sermon applies to teenagers, students hear that worship is about the adults and that the young people are invited guests to *their* meeting.

Encourage Families to Worship Together

Are we actively encouraging families to worship together? Are there programs or patterns that prohibit families from worshiping together? I can think of few worse ideas than having a youth service run concurrently with the main worship service, such that teenagers are separated from the rest of the congregation.

Develop an Intergenerational Group of Youth Leaders

Does the youth ministry team reflect a variety of ages? Young adults who work with students don't have much life experience. Older leaders will help connect the age gaps in a church.

Encourage Older Adults to Initiate with Youth

Are older adults encouraged to reach out to youth? We cannot expect students to initiate relationships with older generations. At the same time, older adults may feel hesitant to initiate with teenagers without exhortation. Let adults know the value of initiating conversations and relationships with younger parishioners.

Host Intergenerational Events as a Church

Does your church offer intergenerational events? These are the easiest and most common ways to connect generations, although they are not enough in themselves to bring full integration.

Looking Forward

We all want what is best for the youth of our churches. God has shown us a better way than the age-segregated congregation. There is a place for a youth ministry in the church! But our efforts to minister to teens must be an integrated part of the life of the church. The future of our churches depends on the way we integrate our young people into the intergenerational people of God today!

More on . . . Integration between Generations

Kevin DeYoung and Greg Gilbert, *What Is the Mission of the Church? Making Sense of Social Justice, Shalom, and the Great Commission* (Crossway, 2011).

Bobby Jamieson, *Committing to One Another: Church Membership* (Crossway, 2012).

Josh Moody, *How Church Can Change Your Life: Answers to the Ten Most Common Questions about Church* (Christian Focus, 2015).

Charles M. Sell, *Family Ministry* (Zondervan, 1995).

Part 2

PRACTICAL APPLICATIONS FOR A GOSPEL-CENTERED YOUTH MINISTRY

8

Helping Students Personally Engage the Bible

Small-Group Bible Study in Youth Ministry

Jon Nielson

If you've been in youth ministry for a while, you know the joys—and the frustrations—of trying to teach the Bible substantively to junior high and high school students. We probably all have had times at youth group when we feel, almost tangibly, the Holy Spirit speaking to young people through his Word. We've also had times when the students are so squirrelly that we wonder if anything is getting through at all!

What I want to propose, very simply in this chapter, is that Bible study–based small groups have great potential for extending and bolstering your overall Word ministry to young people as a youth leader, director, or pastor. I want to suggest that a vibrant and thoughtful commitment to directing and organizing small group

Bible studies in your youth ministry is not only possible, but even *necessary* for your students, in order to help them grow deeper in their knowledge of God's Word and the gospel of Jesus Christ.

Biblical and Theological Foundations

Tom Olson, in his excellent chapter on worship through music in this book (chapter 10), builds much of his foundation for his arguments and suggestions on the following passage from Colossians 3:

> Let the word of Christ dwell in you richly, teaching and admonishing one another in all wisdom, singing psalms and hymns and spiritual songs, with thankfulness in your hearts to God. And whatever you do, in word or deed, do everything in the name of the Lord Jesus, giving thanks to God the Father through him. (3:16–17)

I want you to notice a few specific points that we gather from these verses—ones that I believe apply to the way we help our students engage in small group Bible studies as part of our overall ministry of the Word in youth group contexts.

First, notice that the call of the apostle Paul to God's people is to allow—to let—the word of Christ dwell in them. People of God, quite simply, are to be people of God's Word. If we do not have this kind of focus as an aim in our youth ministry, then we are after something different than what was put forward as a goal by the apostles themselves.

Second, notice the command in verse 16 that Christians are to teach and admonish one another, based on the Word of God. In fact, it seems as if the "teaching" and "admonishing" that Paul is saying should be going on in the church is actually a *way* in which Christians allow the word of Christ to dwell richly in them! Now, there are plenty of places in the New Testament where Paul calls pastors and elders to teach and preach the Word to God's people in the church. This passage in Colossians 3, though, is a call for "regular" Christians in the church (nonpastors and nonelders included), to be active in teaching each other the word of Christ and the truths of the biblical gospel.

I want to argue, then, that unless your Word ministry as a youth director or pastor *extends beyond your public teaching of the youth group into the interpersonal relationships of your students*, you are actually failing to allow the command of Paul in Colossians 3 to come to full fruition in your youth ministry. Let me put this a slightly different way. Teaching the Bible from "up front" is great; figuring out how to get the Bible taught and applied on a relational level between and among your students—in addition to up-front teaching—makes your overall Word ministry far stronger. It is my conviction that this interpersonal teaching and admonishment from God's Word can happen brilliantly in the context of small group Bible studies within the youth ministry.

Really, what I am arguing for has at its root the important, gospel-grounded idea, started by Martin Luther, of what we now call the "priesthood of all believers."[1] This, in simple terms, means that because of the work of Jesus Christ on the cross, every genuine believer in him has equal access to God the Father through the blood of the Savior. The Holy Spirit indwells every believer in Jesus, enabling each one to understand his inspired Word, believe it, and even speak it and apply it faithfully to the lives of friends and family members. This does not, in any way, minimize the significance of the office of pastor and elder—men whom the church has laid hands on and ordained for the work of gospel ministry. Preaching and teaching is a wonderful gift as well as a high calling from God! What this does mean, though, is that youth directors and pastors do not have a monopoly on Word ministry. According to Paul, Word ministry is meant to be happening all the time—believer to believer—as the Word of God is spoken, taught, applied, and brought to bear on people's lives throughout the week. Friends, well-run and thoughtfully designed small group Bible studies, in the context of a Word-centered youth ministry, can contribute to this

---

[1] Martin Luther, *To The Christian Nobility of the German Nation* (1520).

ongoing and comprehensive ministry of the Word—even among young people!

A Brief Story

This year in our student ministry at church, we have seen a brilliant example of this. One young man, who has sat through many of my Sunday morning messages (in which I try, to the best of my ability, to proclaim Christ and his gospel faithfully and clearly), began attending a student-led small group. I had directed the small groups to study the book of Ephesians, meeting with the small group leaders regularly to help them with leadership and providing them with some preparation materials and discussion questions to ask as they led their respective groups. In the context of a family's living room, with a dozen or so students huddled around Ephesians 2, this young man (who had been raised in a Roman Catholic family and had not read the Bible regularly himself), understood the gospel of grace for the very first time. His peers gently explained this glorious good news to him; he was "dead" in sin and under the "wrath" of God (Eph. 2:1–3); in Christ, God could raise him to life if he accepted the free offer of God's grace through the death and resurrection of his perfect Son through faith alone (Eph. 2:4–10). He got it. The student leaders recounted to me later the look of amazement that came over his face, as he realized the gracious offer of God, which could only be received by faith. His works had never been enough, and he had known it all along. Smiling broadly, this young man "got" grace through the living room–based, small-group enabled ministry of the Word from his peers.

Do you begin to see what I mean? My "up-front" Word ministry had been faithful, but the outer circles of our Word ministry—extended and applied through small group Bible studies—had been the means that God used to bring this young man to a full understanding of the gospel. A dozen students huddled around the book of Ephesians, asking questions. And God spoke his Word and his truth to this young man.

Getting "Deep" in Small Group?

Now, if your experience in youth ministry has been anything like mine, you know that figuring out how to organize small groups can be a tough issue to navigate. Student leaders and adult leaders have come to me in the past, questioning a commitment to Bible study–based small groups and suggesting that this does not provide the opportunity for students to get "real"—to really share the deep struggles and problems that are going on in their lives.

Now, before I respond to this ever-present tension about small groups, let me say this very clearly: students—and adults—must get real in Bible study! In fact, if small groups never get to the point of genuine vulnerability, sharing, confession, accountability, and sometimes even tears and hugs, then we have not really connected deeply as human beings who are part of the body of Christ together. Small groups need to get deep!

But it is my conviction that Bible study–based small groups, done the right way, actually help people get deep in the right way, with a focus on the right things. Let me explain what I mean.

Many people—and perhaps all people in some ways—have a desire to share deeply with others in small group settings. They want to share their struggles. They want to welcome prayer from other believers for their sin, doubts, and trying circumstances. The danger is, though, that small groups that *begin* there (by simply focusing on sharing and getting real with one another) can actually begin to be driven by human issues—felt needs—rather than the truths of God's Word that our God longs for us to grasp and apply to the very situations with which we struggle! To put it in slightly different terms, we often come to a small group thinking we know what we need from the meeting; sometimes, though, God has a different agenda because he needs to teach us something from his Word that we didn't even know we needed. To start with the Word—with a commitment to Bible study—in small groups is to let God set the agenda.

You've got to make it to getting deep, but you do that as you are led by all that God wants to teach, apply, and bring conviction about. In Bible study, we are saying boldly that what we all need the most is for God to speak to us his Word of truth—into all of our struggles, circumstances, sins, and doubts. Now, I want to talk a little more about what this can actually look like in a youth ministry.

PRACTICAL CONSIDERATIONS FOR SMALL-GROUP BIBLE STUDY IN YOUTH MINISTRY

The following suggestions that I want to offer you now have been gathered through several years of experience in youth and student ministry. I've been involved in excellent youth small-group Bible studies, and I've been in some pretty awkward and ineffective ones as well. What I'm going to share with you is a summary of the most important lessons I've learned, and I pray that this practical advice will be helpful to you as you make a commitment to include small group Bible studies as an extension of your Word ministry to your students. So, here are some tips as you dive in.

Train Your Leaders

This is, by far, the most important commitment you can make, which will have the biggest impact on the health and depth of small-group Bible studies in your ministry. Train your leaders—students and/or adults—in how to lead a Bible study well. Well-trained leaders are the single biggest factor in whether or not a small-group Bible study is energetic, engaging, and interactive . . . or boring, awkward, and merely cerebral.

Make no mistake, leading a small-group Bible study is a *skill*. Sadly, it is a skill that even many pastors and directors do not have! Many pastors can give a brilliant and winsome sermon from the pulpit but have never worked to hone their ability to guide a conversation, involve and engage everyone in the room, and lead a group through a study of a passage of Scripture without dominating the discussion or letting things run wild. It takes time and work to become a good small-group leader!

Because of this, the best way that you can train your leaders to grow in this skill is to grow in it yourself. Let me suggest that you do this by making at least a good portion of your leader meetings a "live" Bible study, which will cover at least one of the Scripture passages that your small groups will study in the coming week or month. Give time to preparing for it. Write out good discussion questions. Call on people, and ask follow-up questions. Work on your ability to guide the discussion rather than give a presentation. Model for them what a good Bible study small-group leader looks like!

I should add that being a "model" small group leader for your students takes more than just the right techniques in facilitating and guiding a discussion. It will mean that you are modeling for them (and perhaps telling them about) a regular pattern and commitment to personal time of study in God's Word and preparation through prayer. It will mean that your life, actions, and the words *outside* of small group time are in accord with your actions and words *during* the small group time. In short, techniques don't make the small group leader; character and a love for God's Word are foundational!

Embrace a Simple Tool

Some people can get a little too carried away in their preparation for leading a small-group Bible study. Commentaries are helpful of course, and more preparation in the passage to be studied will never hurt. When it comes to the actual small-group Bible study, though, it will be best to embrace a very simple tool for study that the group as a whole can easily grasp, use, and apply on its own. It can be good, at higher levels of youth ministry, for small-group leaders to write their own discussion questions (this helps them really dig into the Scripture text), but generally a group will do well with a simple scheme for going through a biblical text together. Here are just a few examples of such tools.

COMA

Many small groups have found the benefit of using the simple "COMA" method of Bible study.

Context
Observations
Meaning
Application

You begin with a discussion of the *context* of the passage—considering both the historical context of the original readers and the literary context of where it comes in the book or chapter. Then, you move to some general *observations*—simply inviting the group to share what jumped out to them initially about the passage. Third, you move into a discussion of the *meaning* of the passage—working together to identify the main point or the big idea of the passage. Finally, you move to *application*—asking the very important question about how the passage makes an impact on the everyday life of Christians.

5 Cs

Another tool that we've found helpful in our context is a simple alliterated model called the "5 Cs."

Context
Characters
Christ
Crux
Call

We used this mainly for Bible study in the Epistles of the New Testament. You begin with a discussion of the *context*, move to a discussion about the *characters*, ask where *Christ* is in the passage and how he is explained and exalted, discuss the *crux* (or the main point) of the passage, and end by talking about the *call* that the passage makes on our lives as Christians. It's a little silly, but many students told me years later that they remembered this little tool for Bible study and had used it on their own to help them think through their personal studies of biblical texts.

Swedish Method

The "Swedish Method" has also been very helpful for many small group leaders—especially those leading groups with members who have very little experience studying the Bible. There are three pictures—one for each step of the Bible study.

The first picture—the lightbulb—invites members of the small group to share what "shone" out to them from the passage (basically just a way to invite them to share observations about the text). The second picture—the question mark—invites them to share questions that they have about the text. The third picture—the arrow—asks the group to consider ways that this passage should point to something in their lives that needs to change, in light of the truth about God and the gospel that the passage is teaching.

Again, these tools are simple. Their point, though, is to help a group get used to the process of digging into God's Word together. They all do a pretty good job of taking a small group through the necessary steps of study and discussion of the Bible—leading them to grasp the main point that the text is teaching and the main way that God's truth is meant to affect, change, and transform the way we live as followers of Jesus Christ.

Link the Passage with the Prayer Time

You've all been in Bible studies where, as the study is completed, Bibles are closed, and the prayer time begins. Usually one of two things happens at this point. Either the group (if the members know each other very well) finally get real with each other, putting their Bibles away and really sharing what is going on in their lives, and praying for each other about those things. Or, if the group is less familiar, people go around in a circle and ask for prayer for sick aunts, math tests, and road trips to Florida. It's this suggestion—linking the Bible passage to the time of prayer—which I believe will help a group get real with each other and also allow God to speak powerfully each week into the lives of individuals, by his Word.

Here's what I mean. Imagine a different scene than either of the two described above. Instead of closing the Bibles and the passages that the group has just studied so carefully and diligently, and shifting to a time of prayer, you keep the Bibles open, recap the main point and main application of the text, and pray based on what God has just spoken about to the group from his Word. The group leader might say, "Let's have each person share one way that this passage has convicted him or her, and tell the group how we can pray for the Holy Spirit to bring further gospel transformation into his or her life." God, in other words, has been handed back control over the group's agenda—his Word is going to guide the way his people learn and pray in response to what he has told them through the Word.

When this is done well, a few good things can happen. First, group members end up praying about a whole lot of things—relating to their hearts and lives—that they might not have prayed about, or even been aware of, if it had not been for the study of the Bible. Instead of praying for a sick aunt every week, a member of the small group might be praying about a problem with greed one week, a need for more passion for the lost another week, and thankfulness for the sacrifice of Jesus another week. This kind of Word-driven prayer will add variety to the times of prayer! Second, this should actually help a group get very real, very quickly with each other. God's Word has a way of exposing areas of sin in our lives—even in ways that we might not expect when we walk into a living room or a classroom at church on a Wednesday night. Again, when God's

Word sets the agenda for our small groups, we might end up praying about sin in our lives that we didn't even know was there!

Bolster the Small Group in Relationship

As you can tell, I've been arguing for a truly Word-centered approach to youth ministry—both in up-front teaching and in the commitment to small-group Bible study. Through deep study of God's Word, and prayer and sharing that is guided by God's Word, groups can and should be going deep in relationship and connection with each other.

Even so, there are good ways to bolster the relationships between the members of a small group, as well. It's become my conviction, during my years in youth ministry, that the Word does the work, and generally the Word tends to do the work by the power of the Holy Spirit in the context of deep *relationships*. As you lead your small groups, help them grow in relationships in any way you can. Have them serve together. Play paintball together. Go out for ice cream together. Everything small groups do relationally is going to strengthen and bolster the discussions and connections that are made around God's Word in study and prayer.

For example, just the other night, I led a Bible study in my backyard (it was a beautiful summer night!) with a group of about twenty students. We spent a great time digging into a passage from 2 Peter, asking questions, making observations, and seeking to apply it to our lives. We closed with a time of prayer, and then all walked downtown to enjoy some ice cream and conversation together. It was a perfect way to build relationships—adding personally to the time we had already spent together in study around God's Word. I think our times of Bible study over the summer will keep getting better as we know each other more deeply!

Looking Forward

I would encourage you to consider what a commitment to Bible study–based small groups might look like in the context of your youth ministry. If you give yourself to pursuing this and taking the time to train leaders who can lead these groups well, I firmly believe that you will find the overall ministry of the Word in your youth group being strengthened—to the glory of God and for the good of the young people you serve.

More on . . . Small-Group Bible Study

Brian Cosby, *Giving Up Gimmicks: Reclaiming Youth Ministry from an Entertainment Culture* (P&R, 2012).

David Helm, *One to One Bible Reading: A Simple Guide for Every Christian* (Matthias, 2011).

Kathleen Nielson, *Bible Study: Following the Ways of the Word* (P&R, 2011).

Jon Nielson, *Bible Study: A Student's Guide* (P&R, 2013).

Jen Wilkin, *Women of the Word* (Crossway, 2014).

9

Equipping Youth for Gospel Ministry

Leadership Training in Youth Ministry

Jon Nielson

We begin this chapter with a passage from Scripture to which I have returned dozens and dozens of times during my years in student ministry. It's a passage that reminds me of my primary goal as a pastor and that I use to encourage my gospel partners in their work as well. Here is what Paul writes about the role of pastors—those who were "given" by Christ Jesus to his church:

> And he gave the apostles, the prophets, the evangelists, the shepherds and teachers, to equip the saints for the work of ministry, for building up the body of Christ, until we all attain to the unity of the faith and of the knowledge of the Son of God, to mature manhood, to the measure of the stature of the fullness of Christ. (Eph. 4:11–13)

Why has Jesus Christ given men like *me* to his church—most fundamentally? Is it to teach God's Word? Well, yes, of course. Is it to provide pastoral care and counseling to those who are hurting and struggling? Again, yes, of course it is. But most fundamentally, what does Paul say that the Christ-given calling of shepherds and teachers is? It is the calling and work of *equipping* the saints for the work of gospel ministry, so that they would become mature followers of Jesus Christ. My goal is to equip—or train—the people under my care for real gospel ministry.

If you have not deeply considered this call—the call to "equip the saints"—as fundamental to your gospel and pastoral ministry to young people, you need to do it now. I'll give you fair warning; this may call for some serious shifts in your mind-set in ministry, as well as your structures, events, and vision. But it's right there in Scripture—the call for shepherds and pastors to equip the saints for gospel ministry.

This call is, in many ways, a tangible way for us to use our ministries to prepare for the further growth of the gospel in our world. This is the gospel that has changed our hearts and lives; Jesus Christ has become our Savior and Lord through his death and resurrection. This is the gospel that we want to equip and train others to proclaim everywhere!

So what in youth ministry tends to get in the way of equipping and training these young saints for gospel ministry?

Using Student Leaders for Successful Programs

I've never met a youth pastor who didn't run at least *some* fun events—retreats, game nights, special events, etc. And, we want these programs to go well! We want students to show up, we want people to have fun, and we want the youth ministry to be a lively and happening place. The danger, though, is that we let our *structures*—our programs and events—drive our youth ministry. They dominate our time and thoughts and, most dangerously, they dominate our interaction with our student leaders (or "core" students).

Because we want our events to go well, we use our student leaders to *make sure* those events go well. We want them to show up, obviously, but we also want them to invite friends, to help us plan the games, and to make sure that our retreats are cool and accessible to students. In other words, our students become moving parts in our strategy to make our events well attended and successful.

This approach is a far cry from the tone of Ephesians 4! These students are not meant to be used; they are saints that we must *equip* for gospel ministry. Structures are never the goal; the maturity of the Christians themselves is the goal. We will talk more about what this can look like in a moment.

Watch Out for Pastor-as-Seer Mentality

Sometimes youth pastors (and other pastors, for that matter) begin to kind of enjoy the way that students or people under their care look to them as the expert on all things having to do with the Bible and theology. They begin to buy into the idea that they have all the answers—that no one else could ever be capable of grasping and communicating the mysteries of Scripture in the ways that they can. There are many serious dangers with a ministry that begins to tip in this direction.

First, the students become dependent on their leader for almost everything when it comes to reading, studying, interpreting, and applying Scripture. They view him as the seer—the expert with the hidden keys to knowledge. His talks, messages, and sermons only drive this idea home more and more, as listeners come away thinking how wise and clever *he* is, rather than how deep—and yet graspable—*the Bible* is.

This, then, leads to a second and even more dangerous result: students never actually believe that they can make progress toward competently and confidently handling God's Word—and even teaching it powerfully and clearly. The task of teaching and preaching—and sometimes, sadly, even ministry itself—is looked at as a specialty that *only* pastors can do in a meaningful way.

Looking years ahead, the third dangerous result is a church congregation full of people (who went through youth ministries with this understanding) who expect their pastors to do ministry for them! They pay the pastors, they think, to do the Word and gospel ministry so that they don't have to do it. And since they have never really seen pastoral *training* modeled, this is a logical conclusion. Sadly, many churches are like this today, and Paul's words in Ephesians 4 are completely ignored.

PRACTICAL CONSIDERATIONS FOR LEADERSHIP TRAINING IN YOUTH MINISTRY

What Does a Training and Equipping Youth Ministry Look Like?

Now, even if you are excited about introducing a training element to your youth ministry, you may still not have any idea what that would look like! The goal of the next part of this chapter is to provide a sketch for a youth ministry that is truly training-driven in the spirit of Ephesians 4. So, what would a ministry with gospel training as its focal point actually look like?

Word Training

First and foremost, my conviction is that training for God's people needs to be explicitly *Word* training. The first priority for students is increasing their ability to competently read, study, understand, and apply the Word of God. Fundamentally, I believe this because of what the Bible claims it can accomplish. Listen to Paul's well-known words to Timothy about Scripture:

> [Scriptures] are able to make you wise for salvation through faith in Jesus Christ. All Scripture is breathed out by God and profitable for teaching, for reproof, for correction, and for

training in righteousness, that the man of God may be complete, equipped for every good work. (2 Tim. 3:15b–17)

What can God's Word accomplish in the life of a believer through faith in Jesus Christ? It can make that person "wise for salvation." It can, when handled well, teach, reprove, correct, and even train in righteousness! God's Word put to work can make Christians competent and well equipped for good works of obedience and ministry.

Friends, if God's Word is this powerful and effective when it is rightly put to work in the lives of believers, then our *first* order of business in training and equipping young people must deal with their competence in handling God's Word! The better their skills are in Word interpretation, use, and even teaching, the more we will see *these very effects* of God's Word in their lives.

Even more than this, by training our students to handle God's Word well, we are ensuring that the gospel will be clearly communicated by them to others. It is wrong, in fact, for us to keep whatever skills we have in teaching and preaching to ourselves. We should share them, for the good of those we train and for the salvation of all they will reach. I am, in fact, getting this argument from the apostle Paul himself; here is what he tells Timothy about the importance of, not only Word ministry itself, but *training others* in Word ministry:

What you have heard from me in the presence of many witnesses entrust to faithful men who will be able to teach others also. (2 Tim. 2:2)

Our local church ministries should be places that are turning out, not necessarily vocational pastors (although we need lots of faithful men in that area!), but faithful and competent Bible *teachers* who can clearly and powerfully articulate the truths of Scripture to this world, for God's glory.

Word training in student ministries can fall into a few different categories.

Study

At the most basic level, every single young person should be trained to study the Bible privately. Even a person who will never lead a Bible study or preach a sermon needs to be equipped with the right kind of tools for understanding and applying Scripture to his or her life. How does this happen? It begins, at the most basic level, by helping students ask the right questions about a text of Scripture—giving them tools that they can put to work in different passages of Scripture. It means helping them understand the different literary genres of Scripture, and how studying Ephesians might work a little differently than studying Judges. It means helping them practice moving from general observations about a Bible text, to the interpretation of that text, and finally to real and meaningful application to their lives as followers of Jesus Christ. There are many different methods to doing this, and I laid out some of them in my book *Bible Study: A Student's Guide.*[1] The most important thing is making a commitment to intentionally walk with your students and equipping them to actually dig into the Bible *on their own.* I'll say this one more time: students *must not* be dependent on their pastors' preaching alone for their understanding and application of the Bible!

Teaching

While not every single person will actually teach the Bible in the context of the local church, I am convinced that every single person should be *trained* in how to teach the Bible, at least at some level. Why do I believe this? Because while the formal sermon may be reserved for a select few, every single Bible-believing Christian must be ready to rightly expound a text of Scripture—or even a verse—in the context of conversation in any given day. In other words, people of the Word must be equipped to handle that Word well!

Fortunately, many of the principles for interpreting and studying a Bible passage with an eye toward preaching it are the same as for interpreting and expounding it in a conversational setting. Give the

---

[1] Jon Nielson, *Bible Study: A Student's Guide* (Phillipsburg, NJ: P&R, 2013).

students principles for finding the main point of a text. Teach them how to read a passage in its context, to make sure that they don't get a different meaning out of it than its original readers got. Help them see the structure of a passage—not to write a sermon outline necessarily, but to see how the passage's structure reveals what the biblical author is emphasizing. The process of getting ready to teach is the same process that every Christian should do when carefully studying the Bible, even if for most Christians that process never makes it to a sermon manuscript!

Leading Bible Study

Another Word-centered area for training is how to lead a small-group Bible study. Again, this is a skill that *every Christian* should develop at some level. Whether it is a local church Bible study of several hundred people, a group of ten in a living room, or just a family around a dinner table, Christians need to be equipped to lead others in the careful study of God's Word . . . if we really believe God's Word can accomplish what Paul says it can when handled properly (2 Tim. 3:15–17)! What does this look like?

At a content level, this will involve some Bible learning in the context of a youth ministry. Students who are well equipped to lead others in Bible study know (at least):

- the books of the Bible
- the basic themes and content of most of the books
- the shape of the storyline/development of the Bible
- a gospel-centered understanding of the big picture

They don't have to be experts, but trained Bible study leaders (even teenage ones) should be equipped with some basic knowledge of Bible content.

Methodologically, too, there is some training that needs to be done. Student Bible study leaders should be trained in some different tools or approaches to studying passages of the Bible. They should have sets of questions (which might be different for different biblical genres) that they can use to get the group to the main point and main application of a Bible passage. Also, they should be equipped with some principles for leading discussion in general—how to ask good questions, how to involve people, how to deal with someone who wants to dominate the discussion, and the like. Teenagers are *not* too young to be trained in these areas!

In chapter 8 on small-group Bible study in youth ministry, I explained what some of these tools are—basically, different methods for leading a group in the study of God's Word. Student leaders would do well to be equipped with some of these.

Discipleship Training

The next category for training in the context of youth ministry is certainly connected to Word training, but it is more focused and specific; it is the training of a student to actually *disciple* a younger student and help him or her grow in relationship with Christ Jesus. Darren DePaul talked much more about what discipleship actually is in chapter 2. Here we will just identify this as a category of training. Students must not just be "thrown out" and told to mentor younger students; they must be shown how to actually walk with someone in a gospel-centered, Word-driven, prayer-empowered discipleship relationship.

Youth pastors do this, first, by modeling these kinds of relationships to their student leaders. Pastors show student leaders what discipleship looks like by discipling and mentoring them personally. Then, with that foundation laid, youth pastors can explain to their youth leaders why they did what they did, their motivation for it, and how the student can in turn apply those same discipleship principles to a relationship with a younger student.

Evangelism Training

It is possible for a student to have good training in handling the Word, an excellent approach to truly Christian discipleship, and yet still be very weak in his or her ability to share the gospel clearly and winsomely to someone who does not know Jesus Christ. That is where this next category of training comes in. Youth pastors and leaders should be training their students to *share the biblical gospel* fully, clearly, faithfully, and relevantly to unbelievers—even unbelievers who have little to no background in the Christian faith. Shame on us if we preach at them again and again, "Share the gospel with your friends," and never equip them to do this well! What does this training look like, exactly?

First, it means that we give them content; we train and equip them to share the *full* biblical gospel. In essence, this usually involves summarizing the story of the Bible—from creation to fall to redemption to the hope of future glory and restoration. There is a lot there that needs to be shared, but it is possible to share it clearly and succinctly! Second, it means that they actually have to practice sharing the gospel—first in the safety of the youth ministry, but then in the "field." They need to begin really having conversations with people who are not part of the church. The only way to get better at having real conversations with people about the good news of God's eternal salvation through Jesus Christ is to actually start doing it—again and again and again.

Broader Approach

Word training, discipleship training, and evangelism training are all distinct categories—handles on which youth pastors can hang their equipping work as they seek to fulfill their calling as defined in Ephesians 4 by the apostle Paul. But there are also some broader ways that students can be trained and equipped to serve Jesus as they grow and mature in their faith. These ways do not fall into a specific category; you wouldn't have an afternoon training session in any of the following areas. They are more caught by the students—as you repeat their themes in your teaching and live them out in your life. Here are just a few ideas for training and equipping students in a few other important areas:

Encouraging Students to Think Globally

We need to train our students to have a big view of the world they live in—and all that God is doing in surprising places all over the globe. The church is exploding in China and Indonesia, where millions of people are turning to Christ and rejecting Islam. There are opportunities for church planting and ministry training all over Africa, where faith is widespread but often shallow and misinformed. As youth pastors teach, meet with students, and talk about the future, they can train informally by reminding the students of all that is going on in our big world. Students can begin to see, in other words, that gospel growth is bigger than their town or even their country.

Encouraging Students to Do Ministry Now

Again, this won't necessarily be an afternoon seminar like "How to Read and Study the Bible" might be, but students can catch the vision from their youth pastors and leaders to begin doing real ministry now. Regular reminders that they must learn from—but not lean on—the faith of their parents will be helpful in this area. Engaging them as responsible young adults who can make real decisions about repentance, obedience, and gospel proclamation will be essential. This kind of training can be caught by students as they realize that their youth pastor expects great things from them as they follow and serve Jesus Christ *right now*.

Looking Forward

You can do this. You may be a youth pastor who has not yet attended seminary; you're feeling ill equipped to engage in Word training with your students. Let me say it again, You can do this. The key is that *you* are committed to making progress in your Word work, discipleship approach, and evangelistic capabilities. As you grow, your students will grow with you, as long as you intentionally commit to bring them along.

More on . . . Gospel Training

Here are a few resources that may prove very helpful to you—resources that you can use in the midst of real youth ministry (which I know is consuming!):

The Charles Simeon Trust (www.simeontrust.org). An organization committed to helping pastors grow more competent and confident in their preaching and teaching. They offer twenty to thirty regional preaching workshops a year, as well as two online courses in preaching (for which you can even get seminary credit). I strongly commend them to you.

Colin Marshall and Tony Payne, *The Trellis and the Vine* (Matthias Media, 2009). This is an extremely important book that lays out the central importance of focusing on building people in ministry, not just developing and maintaining structures. It is a great book to shape a ministry that is truly focused on training.

Jon Nielson, *Bible Study: A Student's Guide* (P&R, 2013). I wrote this book to help train youth leaders and young people to study the Bible in the context of small groups and to actually lead others in this same pursuit. It is meant to be very accessible—a practical help in training young people to be more competent and confident in the study of God's Word.

10

Singing That Flows from the Gospel

Music in Youth Ministry

Tom Olson

In college, I took my first paid position in youth ministry. The church I was attending asked me to be the "Junior High Ministry Worship Intern." What a prestigious title! I was asked to serve because I could play guitar and sing and because I loved Jesus. But that was pretty much it. I had no training in leading worship.

Wonderfully, from that unprepared place, God has helped me learn to use music for the sake of the gospel in the lives of students. I've had many mistakes and struggles because, as you surely know, it's often hard to find the right "note" for music in the church. Yet we can't be deterred and discouraged by these challenges because through music God has given us a tremendous opportunity to serve and shape students for Christ.

Over the years, the greatest lesson I've learned is how important it is to have a strong foundation in what the Bible says about music if we are to use it to its full potential with students. So let's start there. Specifically, I have become convinced that Colossians 3:16 is the key passage in leading us into a joyful, substantive, and impactful use of music in youth ministry.

Let the word of Christ dwell in you richly, teaching and admonishing one another in all wisdom, singing psalms and hymns and spiritual songs, with thankfulness in your hearts to God. (Col. 3:16)

Theological and Biblical Groundwork

As we begin, see that *this call to singing flows from the gospel*. Look at Colossians 3. If you trace its logic, what you find is that *everything* from verse 5 forward is a response to the gospel proclaimed in verses 1–4. We have been raised with Christ, our Savior and Lord who sits at God's right hand (v. 1). We are hidden with Christ in God (v. 3). We will appear with Jesus in glory (v. 4). So, Colossians 3:5–17 displays the life of the person transformed by the gospel.

It's no surprise, then, that all of heaven is singing the gospel! In Revelation, John hears all the creatures and elders of heaven singing, "Worthy is the Lamb who was slain!" (Rev. 5:12). Further, when we get to heaven, we will sing the gospel too. John hears the great multitude sing: "Salvation belongs to our God who sits on the throne, and to the Lamb!" (Rev. 7:10).

Colossians 3:16 flows from the gospel.

So let's dig in to that verse. For starters, its structure is really important. Colossians 3:16 begins with a command: "Let the word of Christ dwell in you richly." What grace! For God's command is also an *invitation* to have his Word dwelling richly in us!

Then come two phrases that are grammatically linked to the command, so that we'd know how to live it out and take God up on his invitation: "Teaching and admonishing one another in all wisdom" and "Singing psalms and hymns and spiritual songs, with thankfulness in your hearts to God."

Do you see what Colossians 3:16 is explaining? Flowing from the gospel, there are two primary ways that we are to let God's Word dwell richly in us: teaching and *singing*.

God Calls Us to Sing

When you sing, you obey. He doesn't give a command about which instruments to use, but he does tell us all to sing. Further, he calls us to sing "psalms and hymns and spiritual songs." See the variety here! God doesn't command only one style of song.

In our youth groups, we'll inevitably have discussions, even disagreements, with students and volunteers about style and volume and song selection. But there's one matter in which we can and should have absolute unity based on Colossians 3:16: God calls us to sing.

God Made Singing Important

God has ordained and given us singing so that the word of Christ would dwell richly in us. Surely, then, he has created and wired our hearts and minds in such a way that singing will get his Word deeply rooted in us; that's why he calls, commands, and invites us to do it.

As youth pastors and youth workers, we desperately want our students to love Jesus and grasp the gospel. We know that the teaching of God's Word is to be central in our youth ministries. But Colossians 3:16 is asking us if we've given proper weight to singing, too! It's not just a warm-up for the message or a means to corral hyperactive teenagers. God has made singing important. Singing is vital for the health of our students and the strength of our ministries and, in harmony with strong teaching, singing will get the word of Christ dwelling richly in their lives.

Sing the Word of Christ

But we don't just sing anything. Our verse tells us that we are to sing so that the "word of Christ" dwells richly in us.

"Word of Christ" is a unique phrase. Certainly, it points us to the Scriptures as a whole, but it also reminds us that *the gospel should be primary and emphasized* among the truths that we sing together. God could have used broader phrases in Colossians 3:16 like "the Scriptures" or "the word of God." But our verse says, "word of Christ."

Hence, our singing should point to the gospel again and again, and what we sing with our students should be shaped by and tested by the word of Christ. We don't just sing whatever songs are popular. We sing songs that help get the *word of Christ* dwelling in our students.

Singing Is Our Primary Instrument in Worship

Observe that the aspect of music Colossians 3:16 emphasizes is *singing*. Sometimes we may have a band, other times strings and piano, and probably, many times one person alone on a guitar. But we can carry out Colossians 3:16 *no matter the instrumentation*, as long as we sing. The collective voice of your youth group singing praise to God is the most important musical instrument in any time of worship. (Don't miss the encouragement here for those of you who don't have a big, awesome worship band!)

At youth group, then, our goal should be to get everyone participating. That's how we live out Colossians 3:16. We want the whole group singing together! There's a place for special music; there's a place for concerts. But the collective voice of God's people is the primary instrument in any gathering for worship.

Friend, if singing isn't yet a part of what you do as a youth group when you gather, I hope you're hearing the call of Colossians 3:16! *Singing is a God-given tool and opportunity to get your students deeply rooted in the gospel.*

PRACTICAL CONSIDERSATIONS FOR MUSIC IN YOUTH MINISTRY

So then, here's the question for the rest of the chapter: How do we put Colossians 3:16 into practice to get our beloved students deeply rooted in the gospel?

I want to answer that question by looking at *the songs, the singers,* and *the youth minister.*

The Songs

I hope you're already coming to the conclusion that song selection is tremendously significant for putting all this into practice. And if you've been in youth ministry for any length of time, you'll know that everyone has an opinion on this. So let's talk through some applications.

Sing the Gospel

This is probably the most obvious point *and* the most overlooked point, simultaneously. Sing the gospel.

It's good to sing about how we love God and need his help. But singing the word of Christ means singing songs that focus primarily on who Christ is and what he's done. Ask: "Are my students only singing about how they love God? Or are they also praising God for what Christ has accomplished through his death and resurrection?" Sing the gospel.

Further, there are many wonderful songs that thoroughly proclaim the gospel. Consider how many songs that your students have memorized without trying because of their iPods! So pick songs that have your students singing the gospel, and it will get them proclaiming and memorizing the gospel with ease!

Think about your youth group's repertoire, too. Of course, not every song will capture every aspect of the gospel. But reflect on the "diet" of the songs your group sings and ask: "Do our songs emphasize just one part of the gospel again and again? Does our repertoire help our students sing about all the parts of the gospel?"

Use Songs to Teach

I love preaching. I believe it's vitally important for youth ministry. Students can handle it and thrive under it. Yet don't forget that a good worship song is a three-minute teaching that our students can easily memorize. I certainly don't need to tell youth workers how much our students' worldviews and attitudes are shaped by music. A recent study indicates that students take in approximately two and a half hours of music per day![1] Let's take advantage of their love for music. The songs we sing at youth group are an opportunity to get our students humming a three-minute Bible teaching throughout the week. Let's realize how important song selection is and what an opportunity it is. Remember, singing is put alongside *teaching* in Colossians 3:16. Songs teach. Let's use this for the gospel and for our students' good!

Consider What Songs Teach

In light of how easy it is for songs to teach, let's pay attention to what our worship songs are actually teaching. For example, in my years of worship leading, I've found that I need to be careful with songs that ask God to "be near" to us. Why? Because it's easy for a student, who's asking God to be near again and again, to come to the conclusion that God is far away. Why else would he or she need to ask him to be near?

But of course, as believers, the Holy Spirit dwells within us. God is always near! So, I've learned to look for songs that comfort and challenge with the truth of God's nearness and to be wary of songs with "be near" language. Considering what songs teach has been an important lesson for me in both helping and protecting my students.

Pick and Arrange Songs for Participation

Remember, the collective voice of our youth group is the most important instrument in our worship together. Therefore, we want participation to shape how we pick and arrange songs.

There are some great, Christ-honoring songs that are hard to

---

[1] Victoria J. Rideout, Ulla G. Foehr, and Donald F. Roberts, "Generation M2: Media in the Lives of 8- to 18-Year-Olds," The Henry J. Kaiser Family Foundation, January 2010, http://kaiserfamily foundation.files.wordpress.com/2013/01/8010.pdf.

sing. They have notes that are too high or too low or they have difficult rhythms. This can discourage participation for everyone but the gifted musicians and singers. But don't give up on a great song too quickly. Sometimes it's merely a matter of arrangement. Dropping the key of a song that's too high or slowing down a song with a tricky rhythm just a bit can make a song sing-able for everyone. One youth pastor I know publishes a list of twenty songs he wants his students ready to sing so that they can put those songs on their playlists at home. This is a great way to help your group learn songs, making them more singable for everyone.

Also, consider content. There are some great songs that so specifically reflect a songwriter's individual walk with Christ that the song isn't a good fit for *singing together*. Songs that function as prayers of lament or with unique imagery can often fit into this camp. They might be great for special music or private reflection, but the content doesn't encourage participation.

So learn to train yourself and others to think through participation when you're picking and arranging songs. This can be hard to implement, but it will bear fruit.

Sing Songs That Stir the Affections

I've made mistakes in stirring affections in my ministry. Sometimes, as we seek to enrich and bring substance to our singing, we become too fearful of the emotions, especially with teenagers. But hear Psalm 100: "Make a joyful noise to the LORD, all the earth! Serve the LORD with gladness! Come into his presence with singing!" (vv. 1–2). Great truths lead to great joy! We have a great Savior, and this is cause for joy! Music is a great way to show our students the joy of living for Jesus.

Now, of course, teenagers can be ruled by their feelings, and we must teach them to bring their emotions under the lordship of Christ. But that shouldn't make us afraid of stirring their hearts with the joyful truths of the gospel! Let's direct their feelings toward Christ!

Use Variety

Colossians 3:16 calls us to sing "psalms and hymns and spiritual songs." That's variety! Consider the psalms on this point. Psalm 46:10 calls God's people to be still, while Psalm 150:5 encourages the use of loud, clashing cymbals. Psalm 136 models simpler, repetitive lyrics, while Psalm 105 models sophisticated, substantive lyrics. Psalm 51 is humble confession, while Psalm 103 is relentless joy. The songbook of the Bible has variety in style of music and in the style and content of lyrics. This variety served the psalmist as he walked through different seasons of life and will serve your students the same way.

In tune with that, sing old songs and new songs. Sing the best songs whether they're two days old or two hundred years old. Wonderfully, there are many gospel-centered songwriters today who are writing great lyrics that will serve your students all in a style that they'll love. Yet some older songs have stood the test of time *for a reason*, with lyrics and melodies your students will still find compelling. Find the best songs for your group, no matter how new or old they are.

The Singers

Many of you have to be "do-it-all" leaders in youth ministry. You lead worship and teach. But for those of you who are working with worship leaders and teams—paid or volunteer, students or adults—let's consider the role of the singers.

Be Hands-On with Your Worship Leaders

As you seek to become more gospel centered in your singing with your students, especially if it's for the first time, *sit with your worship leaders* and work through Colossians 3:16. Share your heart and your vision. Hear their heart for music. Don't be discouraged if you don't click on this right away. For most worship leaders, they will come to deeply value that you take their role so seriously.

Find two or three awesome songs that you want your students singing and inspire them with those examples. There's often a lot of discouragement for the singers when the songs they used to love picking don't survive your new song selection criteria. But seeing and experiencing the truth of Colossians 3:16 through an excellent song will go a long way with your worship leaders.

Encourage them frequently and specifically. Leading music in youth group takes a lot of time, especially when the youth pastor wants to give feedback on song selection! Remember, many youth-group worship leaders, like me, were thrown into the deep end with little or no training on a biblical vision for worship. Be patient. Encourage them often with specific affirmations: "What a creative arrangement." "I liked how you had us end a cappella—powerful." "You found a great new song."

Pursue Excellence That Serves Participation

Psalm 33:3 calls us to musical excellence: "Sing to him a new song; *play skillfully* on the strings, with loud shouts." We should absolutely pursue wonderful musicianship among our worship leaders and teams. God has gifted them, and we should want them to steward their gifts well!

Yet you and I know excellence can be either a help or a distraction to students.

Let's think through an electric guitar solo at the beginning of a song. Often, a well-played solo builds anticipation, rallying and readying students for the song they're about to sing. Excellence becomes a "call to worship," so to speak.

Then there are times when that solo is played so poorly that it distracts from the singing. That's one reason why we want to pursue excellence. Yet, other times the solo is played well, but it's still a distraction. Maybe it went on too long, or maybe the student was trying to gain attention. In these cases, the attention was on the worship band instead of Christ.

Coach your worship leaders and teams to ask themselves: "Is our excellence serving participation? Is our excellence helping the students focus on Christ or on us?" In doing so, you'll protect the band from the distraction of trying harder to be awesome instead of trying to help the youth group participate. Help your worship teams, and you'll help your whole youth group.

Involve Students as Much as You Can

Oftentimes, a serviceable student band will be better than a top-notch adult band, because students are drawn by their peers to participate. A senior guy leading by singing his guts out to Christ will often shake a freshman boy out of the view that singing is lame. This doesn't contradict any points on excellence. Simply, students have a unique, God-given influence on their peers. So involve students as much as you can.

Not only that, but worship leading and worship bands are *a great leadership lab for your students*, where you can take them to a greater depth and maturity in their walk with Christ. They're in a situation where they're ready to be challenged with questions like: "What are the responsibilities and challenges of public ministry?" "What kind of character does God desire in those who lead his people?" "Is the goal of being in the band popularity or serving the youth group for the glory of God?"

Yes, there are challenges with student participation. But when students see their peers rejoicing in the gospel through song, it's absolutely contagious.

The Youth Minister

As we close, let's think about you, the youth pastor. Or, maybe you're the volunteer leader for your group. In either case, let's think about the person that the students and church identify as the leader of the youth group. If you're that person . . .

Sing Yourself! Be Engaged!

When you're in the front row singing at the top of your lungs, students will follow your lead and discover the joy of singing praise to Christ.

But when you're fiddling around with your message notes in the back or when you're talking to your volunteers during the singing, you're implicitly teaching students that singing doesn't matter so much.

So get all your details—PowerPoint, message notes, volunteer conversations—settled before it is time to sing. I learned this from my childhood pastor. I don't remember many of the songs we sang, but I do remember him belting those songs out in the front row. His example changed me. More than twenty-five years later, I still remember it.

Youth pastors and youth leaders, let's sing!

Teach on Singing

Take a week, maybe even two or three, to teach your students about singing. It's something they'll do for the rest of their lives in the church.

Teach them that God commands, calls, and invites us to sing. Teach them how it helps the word of Christ dwell richly in them. Teach them the joy they can find in their faith when they participate.

Remember, many people have not thought deeply about what the Bible says about singing. That's my own story. So when you teach on it, you're unveiling the joys God has invited us into when we sing the word of Christ together.

Looking Forward

Friend, when the songs, the singers, and the youth minister are in harmony, the Lord will impact our students greatly through music. May we lead well in seeing the word of Christ dwell richly and joyfully within them!

More on . . . Music

Bob Kauflin, *Worship Matters: Leading Others to Encounter the Greatness of God* (Crossway, 2008).

D. A. Carson, Timothy Keller, Mark Ashton, and R. Kent Hughes, *Worship by the Book* (Zondervan, 2002).

11

Interrupting the Regular Routine

Retreats and Events in Youth Ministry

Jason Draper

I can remember one of my first big events as a youth leader. I remember my excitement and zeal. As a Christian school chaplain, I had planned what I thought would be an amazing event to build up the parents of our students. I flew in a very well-known pastor and author from out of town to speak on biblical parenting. He agreed to come, with the understanding that there were over fifteen hundred kids in our school, so there was the potential that hundreds of parents would be there. I was not at all prepared for an event of this magnitude, however, and the preparation was very inadequate. It lacked collaboration; I didn't form a team for the planning or execution of the event. This translated into poor communication with parents who received very little information about the event.

Details, such as hospitality and a schedule for our guest, were also handled poorly. We ended up with the relatively unimpressive attendance of about one hundred parents and lacked the impact I had hoped for. I learned my lesson!

A good retreat or event is anything but routine and easy. It takes detailed planning, hard work, and collaboration. Even when we plan well, it often doesn't go off like we imagined, and it leaves those most invested tired and worn out in the end. So why do events and retreats at all? Is there a really good reason to make the effort and sacrifice? I believe there is, but we need to have a redemptive vision with a greater purpose than simply offering a "cool" event or a "mountaintop" experience. We need the gospel to inform our big retreats and events in youth ministry.

Purpose of Retreats and Events

To Share the Gospel with the Lost as Well as Believers

A central purpose of retreats is simply to proclaim the gospel, both to the lost and the saved. When Paul tells the Corinthians that the gospel was delivered "as of first importance," he reminds them that this is the gospel that they received, that they stand in, and in which they are *being saved* (1 Cor. 15:1–3). The gospel is a message of salvation not only for the initial moment of rebirth but also for a lifetime of sanctification. This means that students will grow in their faith, love, and knowledge of Jesus Christ primarily through the central message of Christ crucified and risen. Students need to hear the gospel again and again . . . along with all of its implications!

After his resurrection in Luke 24, Jesus made clear that *all* Scripture was pointing to him and the acts of his death and resurrection (Luke 24:27, 44). No retreat or event should ever be void of explicit teaching about Jesus. This does not mean that we preach the exact same message in everything we do to the point of becoming repetitious and mundane. On the contrary, every message we preach is an opportunity to be strengthened by a new textual perspective on the gospel. Every new theme we communicate is an opportunity to stress a fresh angle on the salvation found in Jesus. And every retreat and event we plan and execute is a special chance to build up the saved and reach the lost with a fresh take on Jesus Christ crucified and risen!

To the Colossians, Paul makes clear that the gospel was not preached merely to get them in the door of faith but to bring them to full maturity in Christ:

> Him we proclaim, warning everyone and teaching everyone with all wisdom, that we may present everyone mature in Christ. (Col. 1:28)

We proclaim the gospel that we might present disciples of Jesus Christ who are mature in him. If we are going to take the time, make the effort, and rally the troops toward an event or retreat, why not have the highest possible aim? Why not offer up our sacrifice of effort to God that any potential lost students may hear the gospel *and* in order that our believing students might be made more mature in Jesus Christ? There is nothing more impactful to a life, nothing more transforming, nothing more urgent than proclaiming Jesus Christ crucified for our sin, risen from the dead, and reigning on high at the right hand of the Father. If our retreats and events aren't making much of the gospel of Christ and yielding growth in him, then I would ask, why do them at all? Attendance numbers, the quality of programming, and an emotional response or nostalgic experience, while not necessarily wrong, all threaten to derail a higher purpose for ministry when they become focal points. That purpose is the gospel preached. The good news really does change lives as students are *being saved*. The goal of our ministry in general must be to simply present disciples mature in Christ. Colin Marshall and Tony Payne elaborate:

> We may multiply the number of programs, events, committees and other activities that our church is engaged in; we may enlarge and modernize our buildings; we may re-cast our regular meetings to be attractive and effective in communicating to our

culture; we may congratulate ourselves that numbers are up. And all of these are good things! But if *people* are not growing in their knowledge of God's will so that they walk ever more worthily of the Lord, seeking to please him in all things and bearing fruit in every good work, then there is no growth to speak of happening at all.[1]

There are many reasons to commit to the hard work of a retreat or event. But, let me begin this chapter by stating again: Don't let anything come before growing students in the gospel of Jesus Christ.

For to this end we toil and strive, because we have our hope set on the living God, who is the Savior of all people, especially of those who believe. (1 Tim. 4:10)

When God Meets His People Out of the Pattern and Rhythm of Life

If the ministry purpose of retreats and events (proclaiming the gospel) is really no different than any other ministry we do, then the question comes again, *why do them?*

First, consider all the "noise" in the lives of most students. Technology and entertainment seem to absorb so much of their attention and devotion. When you also consider family life, school, and other activities, today's Christian student often has very little time to devote to the Lord. Even students who avoid some of the busyness and amusement can simply get caught up in the routine and repetition of life and become numb to spiritual matters. God uses retreats and events to break up the routine and invade the mundane . . . often to the great spiritual benefit of students who need to be awakened to the truths of the gospel.

Consider the many biblical accounts where everyday routine is interrupted by an encounter or message from the Lord: Moses tending sheep in Exodus 3, Gideon at the winepress in Judges 6, Samuel ministering in the temple in 1 Samuel 3, David tending sheep in

---

[1] Colin Marshall and Tony Payne, *The Trellis and the Vine* (Waterloo, Australia: Matthias Media, 2009), 82.

1 Samuel 16, and Saul on the road to Damascus in Acts 9. Also, Jesus interrupted the everyday occupations of several young men to call them to follow him as disciples (Mark 1:16–20).

Similarly, Mark tells us that when the disciples had become so busy with ministry, Jesus instructed them to come away to a desolate place for rest (Mark 6:31). When a routine is interrupted or an everyday scene is changed, mental rest and meditation can happen, and special, focused attention can be gained. It is at those times that the often-heard gospel message and call can be used by the Lord to penetrate the heart more deeply.

There is value in providing a time when an environment is uniquely set to minimize the distractions of life. I'm not suggesting any emotional manipulation or coercion—transformation comes through the hearing of the Word with the help of the Holy Spirit. We should never try to manipulate hearts. Yet God does use our efforts and planning to deliver his Word with excellence, and a scene change is a great place to start.

With all of this in mind, I want to call you to pay attention to the following principles in order to take full advantage of that scene change that can happen on a retreat or during a special event.

PRACTICAL CONSIDERATIONS FOR RETREATS AND EVENTS

Set a Goal

Too often ministries can fall into the trap of going through the motions without remembering the kingdom significance of each event in ministry. After all, you never know when the Lord God might see fit to give a young man or woman the gift of faith for the very first time!

Begin by setting a very clear goal. The purpose always revolves around the proclamation of the gospel, but what is your unique plan or setting for proclaiming the unchanging gospel? In other words, what is your unique aim for your retreat or event? Do you want to have a retreat simply so that you can break the everyday routine? Do you want to have a retreat to begin a new ministry season or kick off a new theme? Do you want to bring a season or theme to a close? Do you want to have an event so that students will have an opportunity to bring lost friends, who can hear clearly a call to repentance from sin and faith in Jesus Christ? Make sure you ask yourself and your leadership team these and similar questions until you are very clear on how this event or retreat will support the ministry of the gospel. Write it down, pray over it, and review it with your leaders. If you and your leadership team aren't clear on the goal, you're not really ready to move forward with planning a retreat or event.

Don't Reinvent the Wheel

You are not the first person to want to have a quality retreat or event. Obviously, there have been other student retreats and events with similar goals as yours. Personally, I have learned creative ideas and helpful tips, such as prohibiting personal electronics on trips, but I have also gained things through help from others such as good templates for checklists, great recommendations for retreat locations, and even the right place to stop and eat on the way to a destination. Proverbs 15:22 says, "Without counsel plans fail, but with many advisers they succeed."

As you seek to learn best practices, begin by talking to more experienced youth leaders and pastors in your area and network. Ask them what has worked . . . and what hasn't. Try to learn from their mistakes in planning and leading retreats so that you don't have to learn from your own! In addition to this, solid youth retreat and trip ministries (such as LeaderTreks in Carol Stream, Illinois) are excellent resources to gather checklists and templates for carefully planning a trip or retreat.

Book Far in Advance

Given how demanding ministry can be during each season, one can fail to look ahead. There is nothing worse than realizing your fall retreat is only eight weeks out and you have nothing booked. Ideally larger, well-resourced youth groups should set a date, communicate it to the church and volunteers, and book the location, speaker, musicians, and vans at least four to six months out. For smaller groups who do not book an outside speaker or band, you still want to establish your date, tell your church and volunteers, and find a location for your event far in advance.

Minimize Distractions, Especially Electronics

Retreats and events can be a time when an environment should be uniquely set to minimize the distractions of life. Students (and adults) can be pulled away from hearing the voice of God because of the incessant busyness of life and the virtual immersion into smartphones, Netflix, television, and other technology. One of the best things you can do (and perhaps must do) is to prohibit students from accessing their smartphones on a retreat. They vigorously will resist this rule up front, but students very often will thank you at the end. They will admit a sense of relief in being extricated from the world of Instagram and Facebook, while having an opportunity to connect more deeply with God and friends. They will find the satisfaction of concentrating on relationship with Christ without daily distraction.

Budget Time for Students to Process

For many students, retreats constitute some of the most powerful spiritual experiences of their lives. Very often, when a person offers his or her testimony, a retreat or event has a chapter in the story of how he or she came to follow Jesus. Given the potential for life-changing moments, one needs to budget plenty of time for students to process what they are learning. Many students find journaling to be a helpful practice after talks. Break-out group reflections can be a constructive, provided that leaders offer clear questions and direction. One youth pastor told me that "solo" time where kids have an extended period of time (30–60 minutes) alone with God in the woods can be an intimate time of prayer and meditation with the Lord. Regardless of the format, ministries need to offer time for students to internalize what they are learning about God.

Commit to Prayer and Clarity

As you are making your way through your preparation with a gospel-centered purpose, a clear goal, and with helpful input from others, never forget to commit yourself to prayer. Do not move ahead without submitting to, and being strengthened in, the Lord. Psalm 127:1 tells us:

> Unless the LORD builds the house, those who build it labor in vain. Unless the LORD watches over the city, the watchman stays awake in vain.

As I said before, we cannot manipulate heart change in our students. We work hard to deliver the gospel in an effective way, but we trust God to build up the faith of the individual. We are truly dependent on him, and our entire ministry is in jeopardy when we are not prayerfully abiding in the Lord.

Two very important things happen when retreats and events are covered in prayer. First, we become more sensitive and tender to the Lord, which often gives us a clearer and more passionate vision. This greatly helps us communicate more clearly with our support leaders. Second, when we pray *with* our support leaders, vision, passion, and even ownership is shared.

Take a Team Approach

One of the most biblical and helpful principles I have learned over many retreats and events is that ministry functions best in the context of a team. Paul wrote to the Corinthians:

> Now there are varieties of gifts, but the same Spirit; and there are varieties of service, but the same Lord; and there are varieties

of activities, but it is the same God who empowers them all in everyone. To each is given the manifestation of the Spirit for the common good. (1 Cor. 12:4–7)

The Lord intentionally gave gifts to people around us within ministry for the common good. When we teach, model, and entrust ministry to others, we edify the church.

It is important to know and understand each leader's gifts. I encourage youth pastors to delegate as much of the task-oriented logistical work to volunteers, in order to maximize the relational time that staff has with students. At retreats, questions and wounds often bubble up to the surface for students. Staff need to be available to engage students at these moments. Having volunteers who are helping with the meals, setting up sound equipment, or organizing the next item on the calendar frees youth pastors and discipleship leaders to focus on the students' spiritual needs in this fertile setting. (You don't want to be filling coolers or slicing pizza when a student has the spiritual breakthrough of his or her life.)

In planning a retreat, the youth pastor needs to explain clearly with detail each leader's role. We never want a leader to wonder, "What am I doing here? Do they really need me?" Laying out clear expectations up front helps each person understand their value in the overall mission. I often have a "leader's schedule," which identifies when each task occurs for each leader, so that they have clarity on their role.

For example, here is what might be a "Leader's Schedule" that you would provide for your adult volunteers on any given day of a retreat:

7:00 a.m.—Help get students out of bed, dressed, etc. Be pleasant, but firm!

8:00 a.m.—Breakfast in dining hall

9:00 a.m.—Session #1 in main building

10:30 a.m.—Discussion groups; please gather your small group and meet to discuss message.

12:00 p.m.—Lunch in dining hall

1:00–5:00 p.m. Free time
- Note: Please use this time, as you are able, to connect with students whom God is laying on your heart. This afternoon is a key time for relational ministry and conversation. Please help us take special notice of students who may be struggling, lonely, or asking difficult questions about God's Word and the gospel. Prayerfully consider whom you might connect with, and thanks for your ministry to our students!

5:00 p.m.—Dinner in the dining hall

7:00 p.m.—Session #2 in main building

8:30 p.m.—Discussion groups; please gather your small group to meet to discuss the message.

10:00 p.m.—Bonfire

11:00 p.m.—Lights out; again, be pleasant, but firm!

Set Realistic Expectations of the Post-Retreat Letdown

Very often students have a "spiritual high" while on a retreat. In an environment concentrated on Christ, they experience God in a deep, intimate way like never before in their life. Subsequently, often when students return to their normal lives, they feel a depressing letdown. At times, they may even have doubts about whether what they learned about and experienced with God was real. Youth pastors bless students when they prepare them for the letdown. They need to remind kids that what they've encountered with God on the retreat is real but unique. They also need to remind kids that God remains present and real in his Word and Spirit in the context of community.

Review the Results

Finally, after the retreat or event, review the results. How many retreats and events have come and gone with no in-depth review of the process and results simply because we are glad to be done with them? Don't let your relief at the finish line rob you of all the important things you and your team can prayerfully learn.

Here are some important questions to ask as you review the results of a retreat or event:

- Was the gospel message clear and scriptural?
- What was done that specifically accomplished our goal?
- What hindered us from reaching our goal?
- Who made a new or renewed commitment to Christ and what follow-up is needed?
- What caused details to be handled inefficiently or students to be distracted?
- What took Christ out of the spotlight or dishonored him in any way?
- How did we handle behavioral or injury-related incidents?

You may be tempted to be discouraged by some of the answers to these questions, but they are invaluable to your evaluation of what you have just given so much time to plan and execute. If you and your team are willing to face questions like these in a thoughtful and loving way, you are taking a big step toward improving your retreats and events—both in their execution and in their contribution to the proclamation of the gospel.

Don't be afraid or discouraged; keep thoughtfully preparing for more effective and focused events and retreats, which can support a gospel-driven ministry to youth. Seek to learn from your mistakes. Continue to trust the Lord in the eternal results of transformation that only *he* can do by the power of the Holy Spirit.

Looking Forward

And, in all of our endeavors, may we have the sharp focus of vision that is reflected by Paul in his words to the Corinthians:

> For I decided to know nothing among you except Jesus Christ and him crucified. (1 Cor. 2:2)

More on . . . Retreats and Events

Jerram Barrs, *Learning Evangelism from Jesus* (Crossway, 2009).

J. I. Packer, *Evangelism and the Sovereignty of God* (InterVarsity Press, 2012).

Part 3

THE FRUIT OF A GOSPEL-CENTERED YOUTH MINISTRY

12

A Public Faith

Evangelism in Youth Ministry

David Plant

Christians are called to play a role in converting people from faith in other things to placing their faith in Christ.[1] Yet professing Christians, and in particular teenagers, often feel like unwilling participants in "the cause." Often there is a lack of understanding or conviction from students, but other times there may simply be a lack of knowledge of the most effective and generous ways to present their faith to their families and friends.

Certainly, there are reasons why sharing your faith as a teenager is difficult. We live in a richly diverse culture with no consensus with regard to ultimate reality, truth, and meaning. Increasingly, we are told that to truly "honor our neighbors" must mean that one's faith

---

[1] Redeemer Presbyterian Church of New York City has always been a church with an "outward face." In 2014, Redeemer reemphasized "Public Faith: Sharing the Hope Within." At certain points, this chapter considers "Public Faith" as it relates to youth ministry. In those areas, I draw from the work of Dr. Timothy Keller and Redeemer's Public Faith Team. I'm thankful and eager to share this with you, my youth ministry colleagues.

ought to remain private rather than public. However shortsighted this view is, the idea of Christian *evangelism*—sharing one's faith in Jesus with others—often creates an internal tension because sharing can be considered distasteful, and even offensive, to those we love, admire, and respect. In my experience, Christian teenagers, especially those living in cities, are lost in this cultural tension and respond in one of two ways: *over-adapting* or *under-adapting* to the surrounding cultural pressures and realities.[2] By doing one or the other, students either stamp out or hide away any reflection of the gospel hope that is within them.

Looking to 1 Peter 3:15,[3] our church (Redeemer) has sought to create a permeable youth community—one that anticipates and encourages friendships among those with various worldviews. In order to cultivate this type of community where one's faith is public and engaging, we attempt to provide a shared space where meaningful conversation around the gospel and human experience can be held. As Christians, we recognize that faith is hard, and so we work to present a humble environment that is respectful of where others are in their faith journey. A community where skeptics are welcome means that questions will be encouraged and all will feel safe to doubt their doubts. Considering one's assurance in Christ, this evangelistic expression stems out of joy rather than a begrudging sense of obligation or arrogance.

Let's look at the reason for being public about our faith in Christ in these nuanced ways, and at some practices that can help us do so as we lead in youth ministry in the local church.

The Great Commission: Noticing the Commander of the Command

And when they saw him they worshiped him, but some doubted. And Jesus said to them, "All authority in heaven and on earth

---

[2] Timothy Keller, *Center Church* (Grand Rapids, MI: Zondervan, 2012), 24. Keller writes, "To reach people we must appreciate and adapt to their culture, but we must also challenge and confront it. . . . To the degree a ministry is over-adapted or under-adapted to a culture, it loses life-changing power."
[3] "But in your hearts honor Christ the Lord as holy, always being prepared to make a defense to anyone who asks you for a reason for the hope that is in you; yet do it with gentleness and respect."

has been given unto me. Go therefore and make disciples of all nations baptizing them in the name of the Father and of the Son and of the Holy Spirit, teaching them to observe all that I have commanded you. And behold, I am with you always, to the end of the age." (Matt. 28:17–20)

If you are at all like me, or my students, then you've struggled with the command Jesus gave in Matthew 28. Rather than producing "Joy!" perhaps you too have found the language of the Great Commission paralyzing in its expectations. Perhaps you've found it, well, not so "great."

No doubt there are others throughout history whose charges have been more inspiring. Compare the last words of Buddha to the last words of Jesus found in Matthew's Gospel. Evidently, on his deathbed Buddha said, "Strive without ceasing." We'd be hard-pressed to find a more appealing mantra for our modern culture. With his words, we are encouraged to discover our own sense of truth according to our own dreams. Who can't relate to that? Of course, there is a major difference between these two historical figures: Buddha died never to be seen again. Yet, according to the New Testament, Jesus rose from the dead, was seen by hundreds of people over an extended period of time, and presently reigns in heaven at the right hand of God the Father.

Here's the point: If we focus only on the charge, "Go and make disciples of all nations," without noticing the One giving it, we will be paralyzed under its weight and never understand how *great* it truly is. When we focus in on the commander behind the command, triumphant over death *for us*, then we find an invitation to a life we would never expect but have always hoped for. The best part? It never ends.

The call of youth ministers is to walk students into lives that they actually desire—lives filled with grace, hope, and purpose through faith in Jesus Christ and bold witness to him, the Commander of the command.

Grace

When you receive an essential but completely undeserved gift, it's called grace.

The urban legend around Alexander the Great goes that in his army there was another Alexander. This Alexander, unlike the great ruler, was a coward. So the story goes, Alexander the Great called Alexander the Coward into his presence and said, "Be like me or, lay aside my name." Who could live up to the name of Alexander the Great? Sadly, the relationship he had with his people was performance driven and shamed based, producing brutish conformity to an impossible standard.

The picture of Jesus before his disciples, even before "some [who] doubted," is the exact opposite of Alexander the Great. Though his charge is daunting, Jesus proves in this passage to be a very different kind of King, who invites us into a unique kind of kingdom. Jesus invites both the brute and the coward into his presence and says, in a sense, "You couldn't be like me, so I became like you. And, so you didn't have to lay aside your name, I'm going to lay aside my life and give you my name." In effect, Jesus places a crown upon our heads as we are called "sons and daughters" of the Most High God (2 Cor. 6:18)[4]. When we invite others to consider Jesus, then, we are inviting them to consider *the* One who knows them to the bottom of their souls, and *still* fights for them . . . even though the holes in his hands were put there by us.

Experiencing the grace of Jesus as King changes a person because he or she now realizes that the relationship is not based on an ability to serve him, but on his having already served sinners. This should produce two things: humility and confidence. Humility, in that we recognize a King who finds his subjects worthy of serving, and confidence because we see his desire to serve us through his death for us.

Because of this amazing love of Jesus, his grace informs *why* we do *whatever* we do as a youth ministry.

---

[4] "And, I will be a Father to you, and you shall be sons and daughters to me, says the Lord Almighty."

Where are we so far? We have seen that the man who calls us to bear witness to him makes all the difference in our evangelism; only in seeing Jesus as our Commander can we be joyful about his command to share the gospel. Then, we have seen that the *message* of the gospel—the amazing word of grace—inspires us to know that we have truly good news to share with the world around us.

Now, how do we begin to practically encourage our students to share this amazing good news about Jesus?

PRACTICAL CONSIDERATIONS FOR EVANGELISM IN YOUTH MINISTRY

Getting Started in Evangelism

Recognize That Faith Is Hard

In Paul's first letter to the Corinthians, he asks, "What do you have that you did not receive? If then you received it, why do you boast as if you did not receive it?" (1 Cor. 4:7). Embedded in every teaching and experienced in every activity, youth communities ought to be places where we remember and sympathize with the intellectual, cultural, and emotional challenges that Christianity stirs up. The tone of our lessons and the goal of the dialogue should be one that engages the culture, reveals the gospel, and draws out the minds of those listening to wonder, *What if it were true?* A community whose entire posture is one of open invitation should elicit responses like, "I want that to be true" instead of, "I'll never be good enough for that."

Reject Tribal Tendencies

Let's remember that cliques are not only for teenagers. We all struggle to form authentic friendships with people outside our comfort zone. Yet, truly Christian communities have always been porous ones, where diverse people have easy entrance and access.

In Matthew 28, a specific group of people who were attracted to the risen Jesus continued to have reservations. In some of the most intimate meetings of Jesus and his disciples, skeptics and doubters of various degrees were present.[5] Therefore, as Christians, we need to reject our own tribal tendencies; we are called to anticipate and encourage friendships with people who have differing worldviews within shared spaces. To be sure, these permeable communities won't happen through programs but by youth communities that live out their faith in diverse, authentic friendships. These genuine friendships become the best places for genuine gospel witness.

Hope

Studies show that no matter what roles they play at school or youth group, teenagers feel alone.[6] The Great Commission is an invitation to "Behold" the one who will never leave them alone.

Behold, I am with you always, to the end of the age. (Matt. 28:20)

The final thing God wanted Matthew to say to the church was that, in Christ, God's people would never be alone. It is an odd thing to say, is it not? "Behold!" What exactly are we to look at? I believe we are to look at the same thing Jesus is looking at. In my mind's eye, I picture the Lord showing his friends his restored hands and offering himself as bodily proof that the world is forever changed by his death for sins and resurrection from the dead. "Look! I was dead but now I'm alive. I've put death in its place. Nothing is going to stop me. Let's go!"

The hope of every human heart is to hear just that. *God came for me. God is never going to leave me.* And in the meritocracy that is a teenager's life, this is good news, indeed.

Two ways to extend that hope to friends is to listen and pray.

---

[5] Verses 16–17 say, "Now the eleven disciples went to Galilee, to the mountain to which Jesus had directed them. And when they saw him they worshiped him, but some doubted." John 3, the story of Nicodemus, and John 20, the story of Thomas, provide stories of about skeptics and doubters with access to Jesus and his community.

[6] Chap Clark, *Hurt: Inside the World of Today's Teenagers* (Grand Rapids, MI: Baker Academic, 2004), 21: "Adolescents have been abandoned."

Listen

One way to demonstrate someone's value is to take your attention off yourself and simply listen. There is a listening exercise that gives friends the chance to consider the claims of Christianity with breathing room. We instruct our students in this way:

> Ask a friend to read, listen, or consider something related to the gospel. Ask that he or she give you patience and trust you to listen and consider his or her thoughts on the subject without responding. At some point in the process the person may ask to hear from you; however, the goal is to have your friend feel known and cared for and begin to be challenged in the faith.

Because this isn't a bait and switch, people may walk away with a new and hope-filled experience: being honored and valued by the church. We need to encourage our students to listen better to their unbelieving friends! Eventually, these friends will ask them to speak to the hope that they have in the Lord Jesus Christ.

Pray

Living as Christians means, among other things, understanding that there are things we are capable of doing and things we are not. Prayer is an intersection of these two principles. We can take the time to be with God in prayer—this is in our control. Yet our friends' lives are not in our control, and they are worth petitioning God for. Doing this with the listening component gives us a clearer understanding of the needs of our friends. Do not be surprised how touched someone might be to know that you're praying for him or her. Prayer aligns our hearts with the vision and values of our heavenly Father and gives us courage and wisdom to honor those people that he has placed in our lives.

Youth leaders, encourage your students to begin actively listening to their unbelieving friends and to start praying desperately that God would draw them to Jesus, his Son, in faith.

The Purpose of Evangelism

Something happened in the life, death, and resurrection of Jesus that has forever changed the course of human events. In the Bible, the message about Jesus's death and resurrection is not called "sound advice," or "thoughtful opinions," but "good news."

On occasion, I'm able to give talks in high schools and present the Christian worldview. There are at least two places where I have every student's attention: when *sin* is defined (something Manhattan students intrinsically know but have never heard named), and when I share the practical implications of the resurrection. For starters, if Jesus rose from the dead never to die again, then faith in Jesus cannot be a private matter. Jesus rose from the dead in a very public way, and since death comes to us all, his defeating it should not remain private information. To not share this news would be cruel. Performance artist Penn Jillette, an atheist, understands the implications of the Christian situation quite well:

> I've always said that I don't respect people who don't proselytize. I don't respect that at all. If you believe that there's a heaven and a hell, and people could be going to hell or not getting eternal life, and you think that it's not really worth telling them this because it would make it socially awkward . . . How much do you have to hate somebody to believe everlasting life is possible and not tell them that? I mean, if I believed, beyond the shadow of a doubt, that a truck was coming at you, and you didn't believe that truck was bearing down on you, there is a certain point where I tackle you. And this is more important than that.[7]

Much of the social capital Christians desire to have comes from living as Christ has commanded us to live. The more that Christians recognize that the "truck of death" bore down on Jesus instead of us, the more we will spend our time, energy, and resources

---

[7] Penn Jillette posted a YouTube clip that was reposted on the Gospel Coalition website. Justin Taylor, "How Much Do You Have to Hate Somebody to Not Proselytize?" The Gospel Coalition (blog), November 17, 2009, http://thegospelcoalition.org/justintaylor/2009/11/17/how-much-do-you-have-to-hate-somebody-to-not-proselytize.

walking alongside others to help them recognize the good news of Jesus Christ.

Recognizing the message of the Great Commission is helpful in understanding *what* happened in Christ's death, but seeing *how* it happened can help inform the praxis of youth communities. The challenge of writing a chapter on evangelism isn't whether or not we are called to do it, but *how* we are called to do it. It is our belief that the gospel is expressed in word *and* deed; message and method are two sides of the same coin and cannot be separated. Therefore, public faith is a public posture of love and helpful service to the diverse communities we inhabit.

So we turn now to considering how to ensure that we are leading our students in gospel witness that involves both word and deed.

A Public-Faith Youth Community

Our vision is to reach beyond the walls of our church. One of the ways to do that is through an inclusive community of parents, pastors, lay leaders, and students that recognizes and believes that it does not exist as a community only for itself. Looking to the needs of others first can help show the power of the gospel. As ambassadors of Christ, our lives act as invitations to a very appealing adventure. It is never easy to have the convergence of Christian and non-Christian students meeting and interacting, but the difficulties and challenges are worth the investment.

Parents

Redeemer's youth community has always been supplemental to the Christian parent's primary spiritual influence. It's from the Christian parents that students learn to appreciate God's Word, experience the power of prayer, and develop the heart for nonbelieving friends. Though the youth leaders provide a secondary perspective on faith in Christ, it is a derivative no different from what the youth have experienced at home. Parents are the youth pastor's greatest resource to know the wants, needs, hopes, and desires of their children. Parents have taught me not only how to pray and plan for kids but have pointed out which friends on the periphery are curious about Jesus, even though they've never been to church. In short, some of you need to consider how to invite parents into the shared commitment of evangelism and gospel witness!

Pastors

When we contextualize the gospel, we are not watering down the Christian message or making it less powerful. Rather, we are translating the historical gospel proclamation for our time and setting it into language that is both heard and felt.[8]

Because we anticipate that churched and unchurched people are always present, the tone of the lessons and discussions should always be one that invites the unbelieving listener to consider Christ. We always preach for conversion, and want all who are present to walk away applying the gospel to their lives: "What if the story of Jesus *were* true . . . *then* what?"

Lay Leaders

Set a high bar for lay leaders, not only as a matter of integrity, but also because of their calling to personal holiness;[9] this is attractive and draws strangers to the Lord. Robert Murray M'Cheyne was a nineteenth-century Scottish preacher who tragically died an early death. However, he left quite an impression on those around him and, because of his journals, a similar impression on young pastors for generations to come. The following quotation is from a letter found on M'Cheyne's desk after his death from someone who had recently attended his church:

> It was not anything you said, it was what you were. . . . For I saw in you a beauty of holiness that I had never seen before.

---

[8] Keller, *Center Church*, 15: "Preaching is compelling to young secular adults . . . if the preachers understand their hearts and culture so well that listeners feel the force of the sermon's reasoning, even if in the end they don't agree with it."

[9] Jonathan Edwards in *Charity and Its Fruits*, says that the fruit of the spirit (love, joy, peace, patience, kindness, goodness, faithfulness, gentleness, and self-control) can be described in a single word—holiness.

You were about the glory of our God resting on the Savior and I saw the Savior's glory rest on you. That brought me to Christ.[10]

To be sure, leaders all have different giftings, and youth pastors ought to look for complementing gifts when building a team. However, the humility of one who "rests on the Savior" is indispensable because, as the writer of the letter states, holiness "brought him to Christ." Holiness looks different depending on the situation and relationship, and often it looks like sacrifice. Time and time again, parents share with me stories of leaders doing small but sacrificial things for students. Perhaps it's taking them to a game, or attending a recital, or simply grabbing dinner with them. Yet it is these seemingly insignificant gestures that are remembered. Often, small sacrifices and relational investments are remembered more than anything the youth pastor has preached. In this way, integrity and small sacrifices can support and strengthen the message of the gospel! The best lay leaders adorn the gospel message in this way and can greatly boost the power of your witness to unbelieving students.

Students

There are students of varying degrees of faith within youth communities. One thing to consider as an expression of evangelism and discipleship is walking these different students out of their comfort zones and into greater spheres of influence, in order that their gifts and talents can be better used in the kingdom. To illustrate this briefly, let's apply Tim Keller's "Private, Secluded, or Public" model to youth ministry.

There are *private Christians*—these Christian students have many close friendships with non-Christians but are deeply private about faith. Often private Christians feel that they lead double lives—one with school friends and teachers and the other with youth group friends and pastors. Any notion of these two worlds coming together would be unthinkable.

---

[10] Andrew A. Bonar, *Memoir and Remains of the Rev. Robert Murray M'Cheyne* (Philadelphia: Paul T. Jones, 1844), 194.

Then there are *secluded Christians*—those who are open and "out" about faith. However, for various reasons, these students only have meaningful relationships with other Christians. Secluded Christians have few or zero non-Christian friends. And chances are, they have an underlying theme of "us versus them" in their understanding of culture.

And lastly, there are *public Christians*; they navigate in and out of diverse social circles, create deep friendships with both Christians and non-Christians, and are transparent, humble, honest, loving, and public about their Christian faith. They pray for the wants and needs of all their friends and talk openly and winsomely about their relationships with Jesus.

Rather than implicitly encouraging a student to hide because of his or her faith or to become isolated by it, youth communities should embrace a public faith expression of evangelism that challenges all their students to live as public Christians, creating opportunities for sharing the gospel in many ways and at any moment.

So how do parents, pastors, students, and lay leaders begin to move from private or secluded to public? Here are a couple suggestions that will allow your students' faith to bubble up in organic ways and that I've seen bear fruit within our own youth community:

1. **Let others know you go to church or youth group.** Though that sounds easy, in some hostile environments it can be much harder than it seems. And yet, even among the inner circle of a student's peer group, other students will know his or her schedule and wonder why he or she protects a particular time period and why youth group or church is something so needed in his or her life. Cultivating a community in which non-Christians are encouraged and anticipated will allow your student the freedom to say to his or her non-believing friend, "I like going to youth group and I really think you would, too. Would you come and see?"

2. **In a passing way, let people know you are a Christian and that it means something to you.** We tell our students that part of being in community is having people see you in dif-

ferent seasons of your life. Certain seasons demand reflection, and these can be opportunities to share with others how your faith spoke into your life. In so doing, you're putting it out there and allowing others to know you think about these things.

3. **Invite a friend to a youth event.** Youth communities with public faith as a core value build programs where non-Christians feel safe. Therefore, a Friday night youth group, a service project, or popular movie with other youth friends is a way to introduce friends to what Christian communities look like and can often debunk false stereotypes.

Looking Forward

Ultimately, we want our youth community to be known as a place where doubters are welcomed and embraced and their different worldviews are welcomed and respected. We want it to be a place where authentic relationships between Christians and nonbelieving students are natural and prolific. If your youth group is known for this, and you hold up the gospel as the hope, joy, and purpose everyone searches for, then you will find that students and leaders alike are constantly being surprised by the ways the Holy Spirit is working in and through your community to bring salvation to many, through faith in the risen Savior and Lord.

More on . . . Evangelism

Dietrich Bonhoeffer, *Life Together* (1954).

Harvie Conn, *Evangelism: Doing Justice and Preaching Grace* (P&R, 1992).

Timothy Keller, *Center Church: Doing Balanced, Gospel-Centered Ministry in Your City* (Zondervan, 2012).

13

Bearing Gospel Fruit among the Poor

Serving the Poor in Youth Ministry

Philip Walkley and Drew Haltom

Volunteers from the church youth group worked long hours in the hot sun and gave up an entire week of their summer because they were eager to show Christ's love by serving Mr. Johnson.[1] They spent thousands of dollars and hundreds of hours giving him a brand-new roof. Nothing was asked for in return because Mr. Johnson was elderly and poor and had a house in disrepair. At the end of the week, the youth leader asked Mr. Johnson, "What do you think of your new roof?" The first words out of Mr. Johnson's mouth weren't, "I love it! Thank God for you all!" Instead he replied, "Well, I was sure hoping for a fresh coat of paint on my trim too."

---

[1] The stories we use throughout this chapter are true but names have been changed to protect the anonymity of those involved.

The youth group worked hard serving Mr. Johnson to display the generous love of Christ. Why didn't he respond with gratitude? In doing ministry among the poor, our ultimate hope is that people would see more of Jesus as a result of our service. But too often we walk away wondering if we've helped at all . . . or even if we've done more harm than good.

We have helped youth groups from all over the country serve low-income families through Service Over Self (SOS), an inner-city home repair ministry. Unfortunately, we've experienced stories like Mr. Johnson's far too often. If you've had a scenario like this, you may have asked: "How do I equip students to serve the poor in a way that is truly helpful and demonstrates the love of Christ?" Even if all of your experiences serving the poor have been positive, maybe you've still wondered: "Is our service to the poor really making a difference for Jesus and the gospel?" We hope to answer these questions and more in this chapter.

The Biblical Mandate to Serve the Poor

The Bible commands that God's people love, serve, and care for the poor. In the Old Testament, God established a system to ensure that the needs of even the most destitute were met (Deut. 15:7–8; Lev. 19:9–10). Micah tells God's people what the Lord requires: "To do justice, and to love kindness, and to walk humbly with your God" (Mic. 6:8). In the New Testament, Jesus commands his followers to provide for the needs of the "least of these" (Matt. 25:31–46). Part of James's definition of pure religion is to "visit orphans and widows in their affliction" (James 1:27).

Not only does the Bible command that we serve the poor, but the Bible shows us that poverty is an issue very near to God's heart. God cares deeply about the poor because every human being is created in his image—having dignity and value. Though humanity is marred by sin, every person bears the mark of his or her Maker. Because of God's stamp on every person, "Whoever oppresses a poor man insults his Maker, but he who is generous to the needy honors him" (Prov. 14:31).

It's clear that the Bible instructs God's people to serve the poor. If we want students to practice a biblical faith, youth leaders must train and equip them to serve the poor in a way that is helpful and honors God. This is a matter, simply, of obedience to God's Word!

The Gospel Motivation to Serve the Poor

Furthermore, while the Bible commands that Christians serve the poor, the biblical gospel of Jesus Christ gives us motivation to fulfill this mandate. As you train students to care for the poor, it's essential to teach students the gospel motivation behind this biblical mandate. It is the gospel, after all, that makes service to the poor something deeper, richer, and bigger than simple moralism.

One place we learn about the gospel motivation to serve the poor is in Paul's address in 2 Corinthians 8:1–15. He writes, "For you know the grace of our Lord Jesus Christ, that though he was rich, yet for your sake he became poor, so that you by his poverty might become rich" (v. 9). This verse alone teaches us three important things.

First, *this passage redefines the way we view poverty*. It implies that all of humanity is poor. Apart from the grace of Jesus, none of us is rich. We were the poor ones in need of rescuing. When we think of poverty, we most often think about economic distress. However, Paul helps us see that poverty has less to do with finances and more to do with our impoverished spiritual condition, which is the result of sin.

Although we were created to live in a flourishing relationship with God, with one another, and with creation itself, sin has damaged each of those relationships.[2] Therefore, we all experience poverty in a variety of ways.[3] This is true for low-income individuals,

---

[2] For a more in-depth look at how sin affects our relationships, we highly recommend Tim Keller, *Generous Justice: How God's Grace Makes Us Just* (New York: Dutton, 2010).

[3] See Brian Fikkert and Steve Corbett's *When Helping Hurts: How to Alleviate Poverty without Hurting the Poor . . . and Yourself* (Chicago: Moody Press, 2009, 2012), especially pages 62–64 for a deeper discussion on how all people experience poverty in some form.

youth leaders, and students alike. You most likely lead students who are affected by divorce, depression, sexual sin, abusive relationships, and more. All of these are manifestations of poverty, rooted in our impoverished spiritual condition. All of humankind is desperately in need of a Savior; sin makes us "poor" apart from the saving work of Jesus Christ in our lives and hearts.

Second, this passage teaches us that *Jesus is the healer of our poverty.* It is only through Jesus that we experience the flourishing for which we were created. Jesus took on our poverty so that we might experience what we were designed for: rich relationship with God, with each other, and with creation itself.

Third, *this passage encourages believers to live more generous lives* as a response to *Christ's generosity towards us.* This is the key to serving the poor that we must not overlook: we must always set our gaze on Jesus and serve the poor as a response to what he has done for us—"poor" sinners in need of gracious salvation. Paul instructs us to "count others more significant than [ourselves]" and to look "to the interests of others." We do this by remembering how Jesus served us even to the point of death (Phil. 2:3–11). Youth leaders must remind students that service to the poor is a response to the ways Christ has generously served us. This is how the gospel begins to shape our response to poverty—spiritual and physical.

PRACTICAL CONSIDERATIONS FOR SERVING THE POOR IN YOUTH MINISTRY

A Word on Charity

We Give Away Far Too Much to the Poor

Mr. Johnson's story at the beginning of the chapter points to a real problem in the way we often address poverty: We give away far too much to the poor. When we do this, we are in danger of creating entitlement.

Poor people are not poor because they do not have enough stuff. In fact, because of well-intentioned mission work and government aid, many of the world's poor have been given lots of stuff. Yet poverty is still a massive global issue. As we saw in 2 Corinthians 8, we are all poor, because poverty is ultimately rooted in brokenness and need for a Savior, not in a lack of money or resources.[4]

Robert Lupton has more than forty years' experience working with the poor in Atlanta. He helps us understand how giving away too much to the poor can be harmful:

Give once and you elicit appreciation.
Give twice and you create anticipation.
Give three times and you create expectation.
Give four times and it becomes entitlement.
Give five times and you establish dependency.[5]

As we saw with Mr. Johnson, giving too much away can turn into a cycle of entitlement and dependency. Mr. Johnson cannot be totally blamed for his attitude towards the youth group's benevolence. In many ways, through one-way giving, we unintentionally create unhealthy relationships. Instead of appreciation, Mr. Johnson began to feel entitlement. He was not thinking about how he could serve others but about how he could be served. This is the opposite of the model Jesus gives us (Mark 10:45).

Creating entitlement is robbing people of the joy of using their God-given gifts to serve and bless others; we are *doing for* them rather than *doing with* them. We are actually hindering them from experiencing the joy that we experience in serving them in response to the glorious gospel of Jesus Christ!

Empowerment, on the other hand, is equipping people as God's image bearers to do all that he created them to do. God has given each of us gifts to serve and bless others. If we are not careful, our

---

[4] Corbett and Fikkert, *When Helping Hurts*.
[5] Focused Community Strategies, "Principles for Helpers," Resources, 2015, http://fcsministries.org/resources.

giving away too much could subvert the good work God wants to do through others (Eph. 2:10).

We Give Far Too Little Credit to the Poor for What They Can Do for Themselves

Once we began to realize the dangers of entitlement, we began changing the culture of SOS to one that requires more participation from those we serve. We moved, in other words, from "entitlement" to "empowerment," which actually served to invite others into gospel belief and gospel service.

When we first met Mrs. Taylor during her initial home assessment, we explained to her that there was no financial cost to repair her home, but that she and any other able-bodied household members would be required to participate in the work either by working directly on the home or by volunteering at our facility. Once we began work on her home, I (Philip) stopped by to visit and saw her in the driveway wearing work gloves and a hard hat, picking up old shingles and throwing them in the Dumpster. When I asked how she was doing, the first thing she said was, "I'm so glad you said we had to help out. I'm so thankful to be getting a new roof and want to do anything I can to help." That was quite a different response than Mr. Johnson's! What was the biggest difference? It was that we affirmed her dignity by *simply asking her to participate*. We helped her know she was valued and had something to offer. She might not have had enough money for a new roof, but she could help a team of volunteers do the work!

One of the ways we encourage participation is by asking all of the homeowners we partner with, "What are you good at? What do you enjoy doing?" Then we try to find ways for them to use those gifts and passions. When we serve the poor without their input and/ or participation, we rob them of the same dignity and joy that we receive from giving. Luke reminds us of Jesus's words: "It is more blessed to give than to receive" (Acts 20:35). Youth groups know this truth well. That's why we take so many mission trips! But if we're not careful, we can hoard all of those blessings for ourselves. If we really want to love and serve the poor, wouldn't we want them to experience the blessing of giving as well?

Is There Any Room for Charity?

Is it ever okay to give someone something for free? Isn't that the clearest picture of the gospel—a free, unmerited gift? Don't verses like Matthew 5:42 and Matthew 19:21 teach us the importance of giving and blessing others, regardless of whether or not it leads to entitlement? And doesn't Jesus give to others without asking for anything in return (Matt. 9:28–30; Mark 1:40–42)?

We are not implying that you should *never* give anything to the poor. There are times this can and should happen. But we have become convinced that it should only happen according to the following guidelines:

- **Give in crisis situations.** Immediately following a natural disaster or other emergency situations, when people have no capacity to meet their needs, can be a time to help "stop the bleeding." The problem is that we too often treat chronic needs with crisis responses. We must know the difference.[6]
- **Give for the sake of your own heart.** Jesus says that you should, among other things, "give to the one who begs from you . . . so that you may be sons of your Father who is in heaven" (Matt. 5:42, 45). In other words, there are times when the Holy Spirit might prompt you to serve someone, not as much for what it will do for them but for the sake of making you more like your Father in heaven—helping you to learn how to be generous and not hold on to all your stuff.
- **Give as an outflow of relationships.** Too often we are "willing to help the poor, and not willing to know them."[7] Getting to know people shows a lot more love and respect than merely giving them a handout, and it allows us to better

---

[6] See Corbett and Fikkert, "Not All Poverty Is Created Equal," chap. 4 in *When Helping Hurts*, 99–118.
[7] Amy L. Sherman, *Sharing God's Heart for The Poor* (Trinity Presbyterian Church, 2000), 12.

understand their needs. Relationships with people to whom you give also can pave the way to bearing verbal witness to the gospel of Jesus Christ!

• **Give as a response to the Holy Spirit's leading.** Prayer is an essential part of charity. We should pray without ceasing (1 Thess. 5:17). This includes the times when we are serving the least of these! Loving like Jesus is rarely easy or straightforward. We must rely on the Holy Spirit to lead us as we seek the best ways to serve others.

Short-Term Mission Trips

One of the ways youth groups seek to serve the poor is through short-term mission trips. These trips foster servanthood, Christlikeness, and community among students as we take them out of their comfort zones to learn and grow. But sometimes we walk away from short-term mission trips with more questions than answers about the effectiveness of our work. In order for short-term mission trips focusing on ministry to the poor to be most effective, youth groups should partner with other organizations and equip all trip participants.

Partnerships

Partnerships with organizations and/or churches already serving a particular population greatly increase the effectiveness of short-term trips because those who are invested in an area over a long period of time best know the needs of a particular community. "Drop-in" trips—when a youth group descends upon a distressed area to build a house or teach a few Bible lessons and then departs with no long-term connection to the area served—tend to do more harm than good. The value in short-term trips comes in supporting those who are invested in serving a people group long term.

Equipping

Training before a trip, learning during a trip, and reflecting after a trip are essential elements of effective short-term mission trips.

Whether you use material from your partnering organization or put together your own material, consider these points.

Train Your Students before a Trip To . . .

- **Remember the gospel.** Your students are not saviors. We are all poor. They are not the ones who "have it all together" coming to serve those who "need help." They are coming alongside others in whom God is already at work, and they serve in response to what Jesus has already done for them through his death on the cross for their sins.
- **Be sensitive to cultural differences.** Just because someone has different preferences or practices than you does not make them wrong. Learning more about the people you are going to serve can help avoid unintended offenses that could hinder the work of the gospel. We want to "be quick to hear, slow to speak" (James 1:19), so we avoid comments like, "Wow, it's so clean here!" (which implies that it should be dirty because they're poor). You should also caution your students to avoid flaunting wealth. Carelessly flashing iPhones or money can be a false advertisement for what it means to be successful. Once on a short-term trip to rural Honduras I heard an American teenager share a testimony about how upset he was when his parents took his brand-new Mustang convertible away after he wrecked it. Most people in that village don't own a house, much less a car. That probably wasn't the most sensitive way to share a testimony of God's goodness to those villagers!
- **Be humble learners.** We must avoid the assumption that poor people don't know Jesus or don't have anything to offer. In fact, some economically poor people might have the strongest faith in Jesus because they know what it's like to truly depend on him for everything. We must be willing to learn from them, not just preach at them.

Learn during the Trip

It is very important that a short-term trip contain some type of Bible study or discussion during the trip. If the organization you are partnering with does not provide something like this, consider preparing devotionals or group discussion times for your trip. This allows students to dig deeper into God's Word and to process all they are experiencing. Often when students are outside their comfort zones, they are more willing to be vulnerable and open to the truth and power of God's Word and the truth of the gospel.

Reflect after the Trip

The value of a short-term mission trip is diminished if there is no change in the participants upon returning home. Guided reflection—both individual and corporate—can help solidify what students learned on a trip. Make sure to provide time and space for reflection to happen in the weeks and months following a short-term mission trip. One suggestion is to ask your students, "What now? How can we take what we learned on this trip and apply it in our own community?" Help your students to see that the "mission trip high" many of them experience on a short-term trip is likely due to the fact that they are being so intentional in serving others. If they will live the rest of their lives with that kind of purpose, that "high" can continue back home, so long as it is grounded in the gospel and consistently informed by God's Word.

Serving Your Local Community

In Jeremiah 29, God calls his exiled people to "seek the welfare of the city" where he has placed them (Jer. 29:7). While those words were written to people in a specific situation, the principle remains true and applicable for us today, as we live as "exiles" in this world as followers of Jesus Christ.

What does it look like to live this way? How do you train your high school and junior high students to do this? Why is this important? Doing ongoing mission work well among the poor in your own community is beneficial to the community and can further impact your students and enhance their experiences of short-term mission trips. The keys to serving your local community are long-term focused relationships and partnerships with like-minded groups and individuals.

Long-Term Focused Relationships

You will not change a community with a one-day block party extravaganza. Almost every year a well-meaning suburban church youth group picks a day to come throw a block party to "serve" the low-income neighborhood where I live and work. They show up with inflatables, snow cones, music, gospel tracts, free food and clothes, and tons of volunteers. Neighborhood residents may appreciate the free food or activities for the kids, but at the end of the day when the church packs up and heads home, those living in the community still have real needs that go unmet. I'm not saying that all block parties are bad. In fact, a good block party can be a life-giving force to a community, especially if those in the community are involved in planning and leading it. In doing it that way, you might discover many talents or passions from within the community, like a community member who volunteers to cook barbecue for the event. What a great way to empower someone and impart dignity . . . and let's be honest, who wouldn't choose homemade barbecue over mass-grilled hot dogs?

These kinds of discoveries only flow out of long-term relationships in a focused area. And these kinds of relationships only happen when people—from a church or a youth group—decide to get involved for the long haul. This could take a variety of different forms. One idea could be adopting a local school by empowering your youth group to help tutor, throw parties for teachers, or raise funds to buy school supplies.

Partnerships

Lastly, as with short-term trips, partnerships are key when doing local mission work among the poor. Most likely, there are already organizations doing great work among the poor in your city. Instead of starting your own program, consider partnering with one of these existing organizations. If there are no organizations doing work in the community your youth group feels called to serve, then perhaps your church could consider starting a ministry program, *with the input of the community!*

Looking Forward

Picture students who began serving the poor when they entered your youth group in the seventh grade. What if you took them on short-term mission trips and local service projects while consistently reminding them of the dignity of the poor? What if they were challenged to learn from the poor and to work *with* them instead of *for* them? What if they were trained to *empower* rather than *entitle?* And what if you taught them a gospel-centered framework for serving the poor, reminding them that they too were impoverished apart from Jesus, who made sinners rich through his sacrificial death in their place?

Imagine what would happen if youth leaders across the country trained students to live this way. Imagine a generation of Christians learning beneficial ways to do ministry with the poor as a response to the gospel—all to the glory of God. Will you commit to equipping students to obey God's mandate to serve the poor as a response to and demonstration of the gospel?

More on . . . Serving the Poor

Steve Corbett and Brian Fikkert, *When Helping Hurts: How to Alleviate Poverty without Hurting the Poor and Yourself* (Moody Press, 2012).

Timothy Keller, *Generous Justice: How God's Grace Makes Us Just* (Penguin, 2010).

Amy L. Sherman, *Sharing God's Heart for the Poor* (Trinity Presbyterian Church, 2000).

14

Going in a Fruitful Manner

International Short-Term Mission
Trips in Youth Ministry

Elisabeth Elliott

Let me guess—you are beginning a new job in youth ministry, and before you can even get your feet on the ground, the topic of taking your youth on an international mission trip has already come up . . . and you're shakin' in your boots. Maybe you've inherited a full schedule of trips already in place at your church. Maybe you're feeling pressure from your head pastor, from the parents of your students, or from your students themselves to lead an international trip ("ALL of my friends are going to Belize for spring break—why doesn't our church ever go anywhere COOL?"). Maybe you are sensing that your students are at a point where they need to be shaken from the comfort of their own culture and pushed to experience the Lord in a new way. Whatever the reason, it appears that you aren't the only one. In 2006 alone, there were 2,200,000 American participants in international short-term mission trips (STM trips), spending a total of $1.6 billion.[1] Approximately 32 percent of US congregations sponsor international STMs every year.[2] Every time I fly to or from my home in Nicaragua, I am joined by at least one group of church people in matching T-shirts, eager to share their stories of how they are going to change Nicaragua.

In recent years, books like *Toxic Charity*,[3] *When Helping Hurts*, and *Dead Aid*[4] have exposed the pitfalls—and in some situations the downright evils—of a trend that, up until then, had been seen as only positive. We have heard stories of fraud, ministry relationships broken, economic dependency created, and local economies destroyed. Many have begun to call for serious reform of STM trips, or even for canceling them all together.

The ministry with which I am involved receives many teams each year. Teams that have come with thoughtfulness, prayerfulness, and openness to God's work being done through them—in whatever form that should take—have immensely blessed us. We have also been deeply hurt by other teams—those that come with little thoughtfulness for their purpose (apart from wanting a new profile picture with a cute brown kid) and seem to have an idea that their mere presence among us should be a blessing. Doing an STM trip with your students is not something to be taken lightly. Frankly, you misuse the resources God has given you if you do not take seriously the theology and purpose behind *what* you are doing and *why* you are doing it, and you put the receiving ministry at risk of serious harm.

Without a doubt, STM trips are in need of serious reform, but we must not throw the baby out with the bathwater. Short-term interna-

---

[1] Roger Peterson, "Short-Term Missions Long-Term Impact?" (lecture, Interdenominational Foreign Missions Association and Evangelical Missiological Society conference, Minneapolis, September 28, 2007), quoted in Steve Corbett and Brian Fikkert, *When Helping Hurts: How to Alleviate Poverty without Hurting the Poor . . . and Yourself* (Chicago: Moody Press, 2009, 2012), 151.

[2] LiErin Probassco "Giving Time, Not Money: Long-Term Impacts of Short-Term Mission Trips," *Missiology* 41, no. 2 (April 2013), 202–24.

[3] Robert D. Lupton, *Toxic Charity: How Churches and Charities Hurt Those They Help (and How to Reverse It)* (New York: HarperOne, 2011).

[4] Dambisa Moyo, *Dead Aid: Why Aid Is Not Working and How There Is a Better Way for Africa* (New York: Farrar, Straus & Giroux, 2009).

tional trips can be some of the most fruitful experiences for students in their youth ministry careers, and they can do real, long-term good for the host ministries as well.[5] However, with so much at stake, we must consider very carefully the theology and methodology that drive our STM trips. This chapter will address why and how we are called to go and give some practical steps for leading an STM trip that points all involved (leaders, students, and those we serve) to Christ.

Theological Basis for International STM Trips

As we consider reforming the way that STM trips are carried out, we must begin with a clear understanding of *why* we are doing what we are doing, as well as *how* we are doing what we are doing. Even though most of my life I have felt the Lord calling me to international ministry, I have also deeply struggled with the question of *why* he calls his people to go. Through much praying, Scripture searching, fellowshiping with wise people, and reading good books, I have found that the truth on this topic is clearly spelled out in Scripture (though at times seemingly contradictory), and I have learned to rest in the tension.

Why Are We Called to Go?

First, let's be clear that God does not *need* us to go—to serve the poor, to make disciples, or to work toward the witness and demonstration of his kingdom on earth. This much is plain: his redeeming work in the world *cannot* depend on us, because he is the sovereign, omnipotent, and omniscient Creator, and we are deeply sinful, selfish, and limited creatures (Ps. 103:14; 51:5). Therefore, *he* is the one who does the work of ministry, salvation, and redemption, not us. *He* is

---

[5] A 2008 study by the Barna Group on the effects on participants of STM trips states: "The most common areas of personal growth that people recall—even years later—include becoming more aware of other people's struggles (25%), learning more about poverty, justice, or the world (16%), increasing compassion (11%), deepening or enriching their faith (9%), broadening their spiritual understanding (9%), and boosting their financial generosity (5%). Others mentioned the experience helped them feel more fulfilled, become more grateful, develop new friends, and pray more." "Despite Benefits, Few Americans Have Experienced Short-Term Mission Trips," Barna Group, October 6, 2008, https://www.barna.org/barna-update/donors-cause/22-despite-benefits-few-americans-have -experienced-short-term-mission-trips#.UwoMraVsg0.

the one who spoke creation into existence (Genesis 1), who formed us in our mothers' wombs (Ps. 139:13), and who chose us before the foundations of the world to be adopted as his sons (Eph. 1:4–6). *He* is the one who is wiping away every tear and making all things new, through the eternal salvation that comes through the death and resurrection of his Son (Rev. 21:4–5). In fact, our stumbling efforts may be more detrimental than they are beneficial, especially when we mistakenly assume that God needs us to do his work!

However, the second service-related truth found in Scripture is that the Lord *commands* us to serve the poor, to make disciples, and to work toward his kingdom purposes here on earth, in response to his salvation of us through Christ. Because we are saved by grace, we are called to go into the world and make the saving and restoring power of the gospel of Jesus Christ known. Who are we to decide that he didn't know what he was asking? We can sometimes say to ourselves, "Surely we shouldn't put too much effort into missions if we are doomed to fail?" But the Word of the Lord stands forever (Isa. 40:8). We must trust that he knows what he requires and seek to fulfill his requirements by his power.

Furthermore, not only does he command us to go, but he also builds and prepares us for it. God has written in the hearts of his people the desire to see the world with all its people and systems put rightly under his control. At the heart of the gospel is the cross—a gift of mercy and salvation to those who did not earn it, but who repent of sin and trust Jesus by faith alone. A desire to show mercy and salvation to those who do not deserve it is a true and thankful response to the cross of Jesus Christ, on which the Son of God died as a sacrifice for sinners.

What is more, this work that he calls us to is real, actual work, with real, actual outcomes and consequences in God's great rescue mission. God commands us, in response to his mercy for us, *actually* to show mercy to others. He commands us *actually* to care for his people. He is inviting us into the *real* work of restoration. It is not *only* a front for the Lord's work in our lives, although it certainly is that as well. God, in his infinite wisdom, has so designed his creation such that the call to go is for our sake as well as for the sake of those we serve.

How, then, do we see God at work as we serve those in a cross-cultural context? Among countless other ways, consider:

- Jesus enters into the world of suffering and decay to bring life, justice, restoration, and freedom. He leaves what is his own and puts on skin. He humbles himself to save sinners. When we do the same, we point others to him and his ultimate saving work (John 1:14).

- Relational ministry with the materially poor gives North American students, who often have no concept of need, a context in which to see their own destitution before the Lord. It provides an avenue by which our ideas of self-sufficiency and productivity can be exposed as illusions. We have much to learn about grace and dependency from our brothers and sisters who are materially poor.[6]

- Experiencing the Lord at work in another culture gives us sharper vision as we look at our own culture—it allows us to see more clearly our cultural idols, as well as where he is at work within our culture. This is an essential skill for students in today's world, as Christianity becomes more and more countercultural.

It is good for us to live in the tension of these two truths (God's utter sovereignty in salvation and his call for us to serve him and

---

[6] "In many of the families I visited nothing was certain, nothing predictable, nothing totally safe. Maybe there would be food tomorrow, maybe there would be work tomorrow, maybe there would be peace tomorrow. Maybe, maybe not. But whatever is given—money, food, work, a handshake, a smile, a good word, or an embrace—is a reason to rejoice and say *gracias*. What I claim as my right, my friends [in Latin America] received as a gift; what is obvious to me is a joyful surprise to them; what I take for granted, they celebrate in thanksgiving; what for me goes by unnoticed became for them a new occasion to say thanks. . . . And slowly I learned. I learned what I must have forgotten somewhere in my busy, well-planned, and very 'useful' life. I learned that everything that is, is freely given by the God of love. All is grace." Henri J. M. Nouwen, *¡Gracias! A Latin American Journal* (San Francisco: Harper & Row, 1983), 6. While we Americans so often paternalistically believe we are the ones with the most to give and the least to receive, the rest of the Christian world begs to differ. In recent years, the United States has topped the charts as the country receiving the most foreign missionaries, according to the Center for the Study of Global Christianity, *Christianity in Its Global Context* (June 2013), quoted from Melissa Stefan, "The Surprising Countries Most Missionaries Are Sent From and Go To" in *Christianity Today*, July 25, 2013, http://www.christianitytoday.com/gleanings/2013/july/missionaries-countries-sent-received-csgc-gordon-conwell.html.

bear witness to Jesus) and to allow our students to dwell there, too. We can be comforted by the realization that God knows his creation so well, and cares for us so much, that he is able to work all things together for our good (Rom. 8:28). He is able to work through us to bring actual change; faltering though we may be, he is strong. He is able to work in us to bring actual change; sinful though we may be, he is holy.

How, Then, Are We Called to Go?

As we live in the tension between our command from God and our understanding that we are weak and he is strong, we are called to go with *humility*. As with all ministry we must approach STM trips with a deep understanding that we are not the ones writing the story or doing the ministry. We are simply God's instruments. We should therefore be deeply dependent upon prayer and the guidance of the Holy Spirit. We should be patient and look to others for guidance and wisdom. If God does not *need* us to go, we should never go in haste or without proper preparation (Prov. 19:12). Furthermore, we should go with a humble understanding that we will receive as much as or more than we give.[7]

Not only do we go out in humility, but also in *boldness*. As with all ministry, we must approach STM trips with a deep understanding that we are GOD's instruments—HE is the one writing the story and doing the ministry. This should give us great boldness, not in our own ability but in HIS ability to bring about his work of restoration. We can approach an STM trip with great confidence that God will be at work in us *and* through us. Even through our faltering efforts, our lack of language skills, and the short amount of time we will spend, God *can* and *will* bring glory to himself.

---

[7] This requires great humility, especially when you are fundraising. People in our Western culture want to know their money is going to "a good cause." They are looking for cost-benefit analysis. They want to hear about how many houses you will build, not about how you are traveling across the ocean for your *own* heart to be changed. Do not give in to this pressure, but pray for the right words to say, trusting that God is up to something bigger than our own pride may allow us to imagine.

PRACTICAL CONSIDERATIONS FOR INTERNATIONAL MISSION TRIPS IN YOUTH MINISTRY

Steps to Planning and Leading International Mission Trips

Considering why and how God calls us to serve him in an international context, you should begin, with prayer, discerning whether an international STM trip is something that your students or congregation would benefit from, are interested in, and are ready for. International STM trips are *not* a requirement for a healthy youth ministry and should never be initiated out of obligation. If you decide that the Lord *is* calling you to lead an international STM trip as part of your youth ministry, consider the following questions and practical steps as you plan your trip.

Where Will You Go?

Don't try to be a trailblazer; partner with a known ministry. If your church or denomination sponsors missionaries, start there! It is hugely beneficial for both the home church and the missionaries to have members of the home church experience, know, and be personally involved with their ministries. If this is not a possibility for your church, get in touch with a ministry that aligns with your church's philosophy of mission and that hosts short-term teams. Don't try out a different ministry each year; rather, prayerfully focus on building long-term partnerships with missionaries and ministries. Always *ask first* if hosting a team would be helpful to them and how you could support the ongoing work that God is already doing. This protects against a design-your-own ministry experience mentality, which is almost always rooted in pride and pragmatism, rather than a desire to form long-term partnerships that actually enhance and encourage established ministry workers.

Who Will Go?

There is much to consider here, and the process of selecting leaders and students will likely look different for each youth group.

First, choose leaders who can truly disciple the participants in a meaningful way. This requires not only relationships with the participants but also cross-cultural experience. Define well before the trip which leader will be responsible for which elements (i.e., Leader A handles schedule and money, Leader B leads morning Bible studies and checks in every day with each of the girls, Leader C leads evening reflections and checks in every day with each of the boys).

Then, choose your participants. It is typically helpful for students to go through some form of application process, if for no other reason than as a sign of commitment to the trip, and also for you to get a better feel for their reasons for wanting to participate. That is not to say that only the "best Christians" should go on the trip. In fact, you may decide quite the contrary. Some things you will want to think about as you make these decisions are:

- Consider creating an intergenerational or family trip instead of an all-youth trip. If students truly experience life change in the way we hope they will through cross-cultural STM trips, wouldn't it be even better to share that experience with their families?
- Should only professing Christians participate? Or should the trip be made available to non-Christians as an evangelism/exposure opportunity?
- Are the students mature enough to handle some of the cultural differences, to eat different food, and to go with the flow? (I would highly recommend saving cross-cultural trips for high school students, rather than younger students.)
- Are the students and their parents aware of and in agreement with all of the trip requirements and deadlines *before* they are accepted as participants?
- How many will go? (It is important to keep international STM teams small. I would recommend groups of no more than twenty participants and leaders.)

How Will You Prepare Your Team?

Plan several required pretrip meetings for participants and leaders. Some topics you should plan to discuss are:

1. The theology and philosophy behind the trip. Invite participants into the conversation about why we are called to go and what they see as the purpose of the trip. This is an excellent avenue for training students in a gospel-centered philosophy of ministry in general, not just international ministry.

2. Fundraising:
   - Will you fundraise all together as a group or allow each student to do his/her own fundraising?
   - Does your church have any restrictions on how students can fundraise?
   - Make sure that as your students fundraise, they are portraying an accurate picture of the purpose and expectations of the trip. Our tendency is to embellish what we are going to accomplish, but to do so robs the glory from the Lord.

3. Logistical details:
   - What will you eat and where will you sleep?
   - What, generally, will you do? Discuss a basic schedule with participants.
   - What forms should they turn in and when?
   - What shots should they get?
   - How should they get a passport, and when should they have it by?
   - What should they pack?

4. Gather cultural information about the host country, and perhaps practice some language together (it is helpful to at least be able to say *hello*, *goodbye*, *yes*, *no*, and *thank you* in the host language).

5. Consider reading a book together before the trip. The book could be related to cross-cultural ministry (like *When Helping Hurts* by Steve Corbett and Brian Fikkert or *¡Gracias!* by Henri Nouwen), or simply a good, accessible introduc-

tion to the gospel (like *The Ragamuffin Gospel* by Brennan Manning or *What's So Amazing about Grace?* by Philip Yancey) to serve as a launching point for conversations and reflections throughout the trip.

What Will You Do?

As the leader of the trip, do not think that your schedule will be completely determined by your host ministry. Perhaps one of the most important aspects of international STM trips is not what happens on the work site, but the time set aside to study Scripture and reflect as a group on the experience. While considering what you will do on your STM trip, take into account the following elements:

- Always defer to the host ministry as far as what type of work would be beneficial to them. Many ministries will ask for your skills in order to see how you may best join in with the work they are doing, but be wary of unintentionally asking the host to create a project for your team to fit *your* needs and desires. It is always more beneficial in the long run to join in with ministry that the Lord is already doing, which will continue after your STM team leaves, rather than trying to initiate new ministry.

- Focus on relationships. Make a point to create opportunities to spend authentic time with members of the host culture. If done well, homestays can be an excellent tool here. Or you can challenge students to have one conversation with a member of the host country each day. As students and leaders experience weariness and cultural overload, this element can easily fall by the wayside. It is important to put some thought into it before the trip.

- Look for ways to allow your students to observe culture and God at work. One of the biggest benefits of international STM trips for me personally has been the way God has used them to give me a lens for analyzing culture—foreign cultures as well as my own—as a means by which to discern how God is at work in his people (as well as the cultural idols which enslave us). This was cultivated by wise leaders on youth group international STM trips. I have seen something as simple as a photo scavenger hunt work as a great tool here.

- Plan a Bible study time into each day. Your study doesn't necessarily have to be specifically related to your ministry, but the rhythm of framing your days by reading the Word together as a group allows Scripture to filter your observations of culture and your conversations with each other and with locals. It also allows familiar passages to take on new meaning in a new context.

- Plan a reflection/debriefing time into your day. If we believe that STM trips are just as much for the sake of the leaders and participants as they are for the hosts, it is important to intentionally reflect on what God is doing in our hearts and lives through the trip. This time doesn't need to be hyper-emotional, but should be led by some intentional questions:
  - When were you encouraged today?
  - When were you discouraged today?
  - When did you feel dependent or out of control today?
  - Where did you see gospel witness, or gospel-motivated service, take place today?

- Finally, set aside some time at the end of your trip, outside your normal routine, for deeper debriefing and reflection. Allow participants to reflect on what they will take back with them, how God has uprooted their hearts, how they have seen him work, and how they will share what he's done with others back home.

Other Logistical Details and Helpful Hints

- Make sure you are aware of all legal requirements. You may need notarized permission to travel internationally with minors, or certain paperwork to enter the host country. Many countries require that your passport be valid for six months after your trip. Do your homework.

- Be prepared (and prepare your students) to be flexible. Life in developing countries almost never goes as planned. Use those moments to discuss how the Lord is truly sovereign (and to practice humility and patience!).
- Be prepared (and prepare your students) to feel highly dependent—whether it's for communication, transportation, your schedule, or even when and where to find food. This is something new, even for teenagers, and can be quite difficult. Use it as an opportunity to discuss our perceived self-sufficiency and the reality of our dependency on the Lord.
- Be respectful of your host. If you say you will do a project, do it well. Whatever state you leave the work site in is likely how it will remain for months, if not years, so be diligent and clean up after yourself. Otherwise you could create much more work in the long run for the host ministry.
- Make sure you budget for *all* project expenses. Most ministries do not have money budgeted for STM projects, so even though you are donating your labor, they will not be able to pick up the tab for materials, transportation, and other costs.

Looking Forward

So, youth minister, don't let the hype or the pressure of an STM trip cloud the true gospel theology behind it. When we keep Christ and the gospel in the forefront of our minds, STM trips can be a powerful tool for the gospel to work in our students' lives as well as in the world. Go forth with humility and boldness, bearing witness to the ultimate work of salvation, accomplished through Jesus Christ and his death and resurrection!

More on . . . International Short-Term Mission Trips

Steve Corbett and Brian Fikkert, *Helping without Hurting in Short-Term Missions: Participant's Guide* (Moody Press, 2014).

Robert D. Lupton, *Toxic Charity: How the Church Hurts Those They Help and How to Reverse It* (HarperOne, 2011).

Dambisa Moyo, *Dead Aid: Why Aid Is Not Working and How There Is a Better Way for Africa* (Farrar, Straus & Giroux, 2010).

Contributors

Cameron Cole has served as the director of youth ministries at the Cathedral Church of the Advent in Birmingham, Alabama, since 2005. He is the chairman of Rooted: Advancing Grace-Driven Student Ministry. Cameron and his wife, Lauren, are parents to three children.

Darren DePaul is a graduate of Geneva College (BA, history) and of Trinity School for Ministry (MDiv). He has been in full-time ministry for nearly twenty years. He is currently the lead pastor at Cornerstone Church in Clinton, Connecticut. Darren and his wife have two daughters. You can read more of his writings at darrenjdepaul.com.

Jason Draper serves as the senior pastor of Harvest Church in DeKalb, Illinois, where he lives with his wife and children. Prior to this, Jason served in associate pastor roles and also taught high school students in Phoenix, Arizona, for several years.

Liz Edrington is currently practicing counseling in Chattanooga, Tennessee, and helping out with the youth ministry at North Shore Fellowship Church. She formerly spent six years in Charlottesville, Virginia, serving as the youth minister at Christ Episcopal Church, and she received her masters in counseling from Reformed Theological Seminary in Orlando, Florida. She authored a devotional for students called *Feast*, and she lives at the base of a mountain with her golden retriever, Bo Diddley.

Elisabeth Elliott currently serves as the director of spiritual formation at Nicaragua Christian Academy in Matagalpa, Nicaragua. She previously served as youth minister at Cathedral Church of the Advent in Birmingham, Alabama, following her graduation from Wake Forest University.

Drew Haltom is a pastor on staff at Christ City Church in Memphis, Tennessee. Prior to his time with Christ City, Drew worked at Service Over Self (SOS), an inner-city home repair ministry in Memphis. Drew holds a master of arts in biblical studies from Reformed Theological Seminary, and he lives in Memphis with his wife and son.

Mark Howard was a youth pastor for five years and remains passionate about youth ministry. He writes for Rooted Ministries and serves on their board of advisors and the Rooted Conference steering committee. Mark has a masters in theological studies from Wheaton College Graduate School. He lives outside of Atlanta, Georgia, with his wife and two children.

Mike McGarry is the pastor of youth and families at Emmanuel Baptist Church in Norfolk, Massachusetts. He is a lifelong New Englander and holds degrees from Gordon College (BA) and Gordon-Conwell Theological Seminary (MDiv and DMin). He loves to integrate his passions for theology and youth ministry. Mike and his wife have two children and live in Norton, Massachusetts.

Eric McKiddie served as junior high pastor at College Church in Wheaton, Illinois, before transitioning to his current role as pastor for gospel community at Chapel Hill Bible Church. He straightens out his thoughts about ministry, preaching, and leadership on his blog, pastoralized.com. Eric is married to Julie, and they have three children.

Jon Nielson serves as the ministry director for Christian Union at Princeton University. Prior to that, he served as the college pastor at College Church in Wheaton, Illinois. He earned his MDiv from

Trinity Evangelical Divinity School, where he is currently completing his doctor of ministry degree. He has authored two books (*Bible Study: A Student's Guide* and *The Story: God's Grand Narrative of Redemption*) and lives in Princeton, New Jersey, with his wife and three children.

Tom Olson serves as the pastor for the Barrington campus of The Orchard Evangelical Free Church in the northwest suburbs of Chicago. Prior to that, he served The Orchard in two different roles—as high school pastor and as worship pastor. He earned his MDiv from Trinity Evangelical Divinity School and his BA from Wheaton College. Tom lives in Barrington, Illinois, with his wife, Kari, and their three children.

David Plant serves as assistant pastor and community group director at Redeemer Presbyterian Church's downtown New York City campus. He formerly served as the director of youth ministry for Redeemer.

Philip Walkley serves as the executive director of Service Over Self (SOS), an urban home repair camp in Memphis, Tennessee. Prior to working with SOS, he served as the director of youth ministry for a small church in Mississippi for four years. He is passionate about equipping people to care for the poor as a response to and as a demonstration of the gospel of Jesus. Philip lives with his wife and three children in Binghampton, Tennessee, the inner-city neighborhood served by SOS.

Dave Wright is the coordinator for youth ministry for The Diocese of South Carolina (Anglican). Previously he served as a youth minister in churches in suburban Chicago and Cheshire, England. He has written numerous articles for magazines in both the UK and US and is working toward a master of arts degree with Reformed Theological Seminary. Dave has been married to Jane for nearly thirty years and they have raised three children.

General Index

Scripture Index

THE GOSPEL **COALITION**

The Gospel Coalition is a fellowship of evangelical churches deeply committed to renewing our faith in the gospel of Christ and to reforming our ministry practices to conform fully to the Scriptures. We have committed ourselves to invigorating churches with new hope and compelling joy based on the promises received by grace alone through faith alone in Christ alone.

We desire to champion the gospel with clarity, compassion, courage, and joy—gladly linking hearts with fellow believers across denominational, ethnic, and class lines. We yearn to work with all who, in addition to embracing our confession and theological vision for ministry, seek the lordship of Christ over the whole of life with unabashed hope in the power of the Holy Spirit to transform individuals, communities, and cultures.

Join the cause and visit TGC.org for fresh resources that will equip you to love God with all your heart, soul, mind, and strength, and to love your neighbor as yourself.

TGC.org

Also Available from the Gospel Coalition

To see a full list of books published in partnership with the Gospel Coalition, visit crossway.org/TGC.